THE

High-Performance

NONPROFIT

A Management Guide for Boards and Executives

Eugene H. Fram & Robert F. Pearse

Families International, Inc.
Milwaukee, Wisconsin

Copyright © 1992 by Families International, Inc.
Published in association with
Family Service America, Inc.
11700 West Lake Park Drive
Milwaukee, Wisconsin 53224

Library of Congress Cataloging-in-Publication Data
Fram, Eugene H.
    The high-performance nonprofit : a management guide for
  boards and executives / Eugene H. Fram, Robert F. Pearse.
        p.   cm.
    ISBN 0-87304-262-X
    1. Corporations, Nonprofit—Management.   2. Organizational
  change—Management.   3. Organizational effectiveness.   I.
  Pearse, Robert F.   II. Title.
  HD62.6.F72   1992
  658'.048—dc20   92-19301

CONTENTS

PREFACE

Directly or indirectly, organizational effectiveness is the focus of many management meetings today. How well is the organization doing its job? In demanding economic and social climates, this critical concern affects nearly every level of management.

For the nonprofit organization, one of the most crucial aspects of organizational effectiveness is the working relationship between voluntary board and executive director. Board and executive must work together in a manner that promotes organizational success. And the development of a positive relationship between the board and executive is all the more important to the survival of organizations with acute funding problems and rapidly changing client markets.

This book provides some pragmatic guidelines to help nonprofits become more successful organizations through the development of a performance-oriented relationship between board members and executive directors. Readers will gain useful management insights about

- New realities facing nonprofit organizations
- Selecting and evaluating new executive directors
- Helping new directors assume their leadership responsibilities
- How a newly appointed executive director successfully takes charge of the organization
- How successful executive directors manage staff groups whose members have different work values

- How to proceed with sensitivity and professionalism when termination of the executive is in the best interest of the organization
- How to handle restructuring mandated by changes in mission or funding
- How to establish employee trust and handle organizational "downsizing" with integrity

As nonprofit organizations grow and become more complex, staff personnel rely increasingly on the vision and managerial acuity of top managers and board members. A board format such as the Corporate Model can provide the foundation for a more effective and efficient organization.* However, organizational improvement will continue to depend on the ability of the board and top managers to make intelligent and creative strategic choices. Effective leadership is essential.

To maximize the working relationship between the board and the top executive, as this book will show, two areas are key—performance evaluation and plans for organizational continuity.

Performance evaluation provides the organization with benchmarks of past activity. It tells an organization's leaders whether people have achieved what they were expected to accomplish and whether results relate to original goals.

---

*The Corporate Model is an innovative structure involving fundamental change in a nonprofit's culture. Its key feature is the separation of policy issues from operational ones, that is, board issues from management concerns. The structure is outlined in Eugene Fram's book *Policy vs. Paper Clips: Selling the Corporate Model to Your Nonprofit Board* (Milwaukee, WI: Family Service America, 1988).

Planning for organizational continuity provides the mechanism for consolidating past gains. No organization can afford to stagnate or to recycle its old problems. It needs to make provisions for succeeding generations of top managers and board members to build upon previous successes. Plans for organizational continuity eliminate the need for each generation of leadership to repeat the same learning curve.

Succession of board members needs to be carefully considered in regard to organizational continuity, creativity, and growth. Nonprofit groups must recognize that their overall policymaking body—their volunteer board of members and officers—is constantly in flux. It is not uncommon, in trade associations, for example, to elect a new board president every year or two. Thus, careful plans for assuring organizational continuity are absolutely essential for survival.

When leaders in both the for-profit and the nonprofit sectors review the challenges of the current decade and look ahead to the early part of the 21st century, their concerns will center on the question "How well will my organization be able to handle the needs, problems, and concerns of our clients?" Evaluation of performance and plans for continuity are crucial factors in answering that question. If nonprofit groups are to continue to meet the needs of society and of their specific clientele, they must strive to maximize their organizational effectiveness or perhaps perish in an increasingly hostile and competitive environment.

The authors are indebted to many individuals for help with this book. Jill Muehrcke, editor of *Nonprofit World*, was an enthusiastic early editor, publishing four of our chapters in that journal. At Family Service America, Inc., Geneva Johnson, President and Chief Executive Officer, and Ralph Burant, Director of Publications, share our interest in publishing materials designed to improve the management of nonprofit organizations. Herb Jarvis, former President and Chief Executive Officer of Sybron Corporation, contributed greatly to our insights on "slim and smart" organizations. Elinore Fram, volunteer director, critiqued the manuscript, and Vicki Brown and Janice Paine did another of their superior editing jobs.

Finally, we thank J. Warren McClure for establishing a research professorship at Rochester Institute of Technology, which provided the senior author with the time to develop this manuscript.

As usual, any omissions or oversights belong to the authors.

Eugene H. Fram
Robert F. Pearse

1

New Realities for Nonprofit Boards and Managers

Management expert Peter Drucker uses blunt words to describe the precarious status of nonprofits in the 1990s. The next 10 years, he said recently, "will see a determined effort to try and destroy the nonprofit sector. We are facing a determined populist attack."[1]

Though he has celebrated the achievements of some trail-blazing leaders of nonprofit organizations in articles and a book, Drucker also argues that the current management standards of most nonprofits are too low. "The great bulk, bluntly, would receive a gentlemanly C or a ladylike D, at best."[2]

Drucker maintains that a primary reason nonprofits aren't successful is because they focus on needs instead of results. As he says, "Unfortunately, a great many nonprofits still believe that the way to get money is to hawk *needs*. But the American public gives for results."[3]

Based on Drucker's analysis and our own experiences with both for-profit and nonprofit organizations for more than two decades, it appears that nonprofit organizations in the nineties are facing many of the same problems that challenged business organizations during the seventies and eighties. The only difference is the timing.

If nonprofits are to become more efficient and effective in the future, they should take some history lessons from the for-profit sector. This does not mean that reactions or solutions to problems faced by businesses are totally transferable to non-profit groups. However, examining what has happened provides a basis for understanding the current situation described by Drucker.

PRODUCTIVITY AND PERFORMANCE

Since the early 1970s, American businesses have been repeatedly challenged to increase their productivity and performance. The pressure for change occurred as the United States was being dragged into a highly competitive global economy. American buyers demanded quality products at competitive prices. The quality of American automobiles, for example, was found wanting when compared with many foreign makes, and sales of American cars slumped.

In consumer and industrial marketplaces, business and union leaders first responded by sloganeering—telling consumers to "Buy American." The words became a part of everyday speech, much like the slogan "Drink Pepsi." However, particularly during the eighties, improved products at competitive prices proved to be the only route to success.

In a similar manner, nonprofits in the eighties, particularly human service organizations, increasingly came under external pressure. Funders asked for more evidence that services provided were developed efficiently and met clients' and other stakeholders' needs. Performance became a key watchword, with major funding sources, such as foundations, requesting more performance measures. Productivity—not process—became a focal point of operations. What was accomplished became primary. How things were done took a secondary but important position. There was no ques-

3

tion that the free-spending days of Lyndon Johnson's "Great Society" were over.

Today, nonprofits continue to be held highly accountable when it comes to achieving results. Standards for performance are increasing in every field. Local funding organizations (for instance, United Ways) require more rigorous planning processes. They are asking for detailed explanations when program objectives are not achieved.

If nonprofit organizations are to thrive, the executive director and board must always be attuned to productivity and performance issues. Very often this is a tough challenge, because direct service personnel in not-for-profit groups frequently focus on process rather than productivity.

The problem is particularly apparent when an executive director is faced with the task of managing professional staff members, such as social workers, attorneys, or physicians, involved in direct service. Many of these professionals often substitute "systems" goals for meaningful productive ones. They assume that a good working system for providing service will automatically ensure cost-efficient performance. Their focus centers on procedures rather than program or client results. For example, those in counseling organizations often focus on treatment modality rather than on trying to determine which treatment method produces the most cost-effective results. This can result in providing a client with a more complex and expensive treatment when a less complex one might suffice.

ENVIRONMENTAL COMPLEXITY

Nonprofit organizations, like their counterparts in the for-profit sector, have seen dramatic changes in the environments in which they operate. AIDS, substance abuse, poverty, and homelessness are just a few of the problems that have contributed to growth in the need for human services. Trade associations have had to adjust to global competition by expanding the range of their services, especially in helping their members take more active roles in the international marketplace. Arts organizations are under increasing pressure to show that the contributions they make are socially and economically significant.

This growth in environmental complexity is taking place in an era of reduced government spending but increased governmental reporting requirements. New, sometimes overly bureaucratic, requirements for report data sap resources that could be better used for direct client service. Meanwhile, foundations are overwhelmed with grant requests as public funds for services and programs are reduced. In turn, foundations have gotten the "evaluation bug" and are frequently asking for more interim progress reports than they did in the past for the projects they fund. All of these challenges place added burdens on the nonprofit manager, who needs to promote organizational effectiveness, deal with this demanding environment, and achieve daily operational results.

COMPETITION

Global competition has forced profitmaking organizations to become more quality oriented. In fact, businessmen and businesswomen everywhere are currently talking about "Total Quality Management" (TQM) as a competitive management technique.[4] Businesses are asking their employees at all levels to think about quality. This includes quality in internal operations, such as building maintenance, as well as external customer relationships. The TQM model means developing quality products and service relationships with customers. It also means developing internal quality through open working relationships with peers, subordinates, and superiors.

Most nonprofits are not experiencing the global competition that for-profits face. They are, however, experiencing increasing competition from their counterparts in the for-profit sector. One finds such competition in many different fields, ranging from day care to education to health services. Consequently, the nonprofit manager must carefully examine the quality of his or her organization's client services. As for-profit competitors home in on certain service "markets," nonprofits face competitive pressures for the first time and find it difficult to survive.

Some of this profit–nonprofit competition will most certainly be disruptive. A few traditional nonprofit fields, such as child day care, may become primary profitmaking fields, and the number of nonprofit organizations involved will decline significantly. In addition, some traditional public-sector activities—for instance, the operation of prisons—may become fertile fields for profit-oriented groups.

BALANCING INTERESTS

Beginning in the 1980s, businesses segmented their various constituent groups and started to balance more effectively the needs of client, employee, investor, and community groups. Nonprofit organizations, on the other hand, have long balanced the needs of such groups. The challenge for nonprofits has been how to manage this balancing act successfully under increasingly difficult conditions. Employment dislocations resulting from the decline in manufacturing jobs, for example, resulted in the need for more human services. However, at the same time, government agencies reduced funding to programs that would have helped displaced workers. Consequently, nonprofit service providers found themselves having to do more work with fewer resources.

Nonprofits also appear to be facing the same kind of internal pressures from employees found in the for-profit sector. Employee expectations are changing, and they will continue to change. Staff persons are asking for more participation in management decisions and for greater flexibility in their work arrangements, such as leave to care for aging parents or longer maternity and paternity leave. The way nonprofit employers balance such changes will continue to be complicated by the transformation of America into a churning "mosaic" society, one that is driven by greater educational disparities, more ethnic diversity, more elderly and single people, and changing family structures.[5]

As always, managers have the tough task of hiring quality employees and making distinctions between producers and nonproducers. As different constituent groups lobby management and/or the board, managerial effectiveness and efficiency become ever more critical commodities. Fostering productive outcomes and keeping the organization from becoming manipulated by various special-interest groups remain continuing concerns.

TRADITIONAL WAYS TO ADAPT

Three traditional methods are used by both business and nonprofit groups to adapt to the challenges posed by pressures for higher productivity and performance standards, changing and more complex environmental conditions, competition, and the continuing need to balance the interests of constituent "stakeholder" groups.

Cutting costs is the performance-improvement method used most often. Done well, cost cutting can lead to greater efficiency in direct service. Positions can be scrutinized and more efficient job combinations developed. However, cost cutting that goes too deep or lasts too long leads to diminishing returns and negatively affects productivity. It is essential that only excess costs be reduced and that all aspects of organizational operations be reviewed carefully.

A second way for a nonprofit to meet the challenges of the coming decade is to increase the organization's awareness of its marketing capabilities. Marketing analysis can be used to uncover new markets or enhance old ones. The markets can be new ones for extending direct service, developing auxiliary nonprofit operations, or establishing profitmaking subsidiaries. These new enterprises may provide broad-based services or, most likely, fill small, specialized client niches. Some may be self-sustaining and require a minimum of promotion; others may be designed to attract separate funding. Sheltered workshops have, for a long time, taken advantage of this type of marketing opportunity and other nonprofit organizations are becoming more aware of this approach.

Marketing also can be used to promote the nonprofit's current offerings to a wider range of clients. For example, a home for the elderly might offer food services to other nonprofits. Standard marketing efforts can be costly if the organization needs to use radio, television, newspaper advertising, or sales promotions to establish new endeavors. Low-cost

8

alternatives, such as publicity and public relations, can be effective in supporting marketing activities if the nonprofit is a community-based organization. However, substantial competition exists in this realm, and success requires special creative effort.

Developing a good marketing program for a nonprofit organization requires a perceptive executive leader who has the ability to assess new opportunities and to take the steps necessary to seize them. Unfortunately, nonprofits too often view marketing very narrowly. One nonprofit leader told the senior author, who was hired as a consultant, that the key to developing a marketing program was a good organizational logo! Other nonprofits have created slogans, hoping this would be a "quick fix" way to solve problems. But rarely, if ever, do slogans, logos, and brochures alone achieve productive results. They must be based on a quality program or offer a desirable service in order to support a good nonprofit marketing effort.

The third approach for meeting the challenges of the 1990s is to make more efficient use of current resources—or, as they say in industry, "work smarter, not harder." The organization must thoroughly audit its current activities and make modifications to improve both effectiveness and efficiency. Though most nonprofit groups are usually stretched when it comes to personnel, it is wise to examine what is being accomplished and by whom. When the analysis is completed, some important benefits might be gained from a modest increase in automation or the introduction of relatively simple solutions to long-standing concerns. In some nonprofits, for example, the installation of fax machines has quickened the flow of important information and reduced decision-making and action time.

THE TASK AHEAD

Without question, nonprofits must change. The security of the past is gone, and the future is fraught with challenges. Nonprofits can learn from the experiences of for-profits and develop their own strategies for becoming high-performance organizations.

Two current business techniques for accomplishing this task are TQM, mentioned earlier, and transformational leadership. High-performance business organizations today use TQM to attain effective and efficient *quality* results. The focus of TQM is on meeting customer/client requirements with cost-effective programs. However, internal relationships are also highlighted as others in the organization are considered "internal customers" or clients.

Transformational leadership is a process that helps top management change the basic long-term climate and culture of an organization. It is the major ingredient that fosters innovative programs and results in a turnaround that builds a high-performance group. The changes brought about by Frances Hesselbein with the Girl Scouts of America are an example of transformational leadership that causes the group to prosper. People relationships in organizations using these two approaches tend to be less hierarchical and more participative.

Nonprofits should be asking, "How can we adapt the best features of TQM to our special situation?" They need to answer for themselves the question "How can quality be measured in our organization?" Obviously, the issue of measurement depends on the field in which the nonprofit operates and is different from the measurement applied, for example, in the manufacturing world.

10

Nonprofit boards and executive directors need to look to the future and decide how their organization will fare in an increasingly competitive environment. Nonprofit child-care centers, for example, should analyze the threats and opportunities that will arise through the continued growth of for-profit child-care chains. They should ask themselves what new day-care leadership initiatives need to be taken to transform local nonprofit organizations to meet the commercial competition. They also should analyze for themselves which segments of the community are better served by for-profits and which by nonprofits.

In building high-performance nonprofit organizations, managers and boards should monitor continually their stakeholders, whose opinions and behaviors affect organizational performance.[6] Such stakeholders include clients or customers and persons in government, business, and other nonprofit groups. In some ways, all will affect a nonprofit's decision-making process. These stakeholders can be either powerful allies or skillful enemies. A high-performing nonprofit, whether it be a social agency, trade association, arts group, or other type of organization, will do everything possible to maximize positive stakeholder relationships.

There is little question that nonprofits have served the country well in the twentieth century. How they will fare in the next century will depend largely on how nonprofit management and boards handle the realities of the 1990s. Also important to the next century is whether high-performing nonprofits become the norm rather than the exception Drucker has found them to be. If boards and managers do their jobs well, the twenty-first century could be an exceptional one for nonprofit service and growth.

11

NOTES

1. "Nonprofits Must Counter Attack on Sector, Drucker Warns," *Nonprofit World,* 9 (March–April, 1991), p. 38.

2. Ibid.

3. Peter Drucker, "It Profits Us to Strengthen Nonprofits," *Wall Street Journal,* December 19, 1991, p. A14.

4. Larry Kennedy, *Quality Management in the Nonprofit World* (San Francisco: Jossey-Bass, 1991).

5. *Changedrivers: Nine Leading Forces Reshaping American Society* (Arlington, VA: United Way of America, 1991).

6. Keith Davis and William Frederick, *Business and Society: Management, Public Policy, Ethics,* 5th ed. (New York: McGraw-Hill, 1984).

2

SELECTING A NEW EXECUTIVE DIRECTOR

A nonprofit board of directors choosing a new executive director should consider this task one of the most important it will ever undertake. The ability of any organization to fulfill its mission is largely dependent on choosing the right leader. Consequently, the board should strive to choose a person whose strengths best match the needs of the organization, now and for the foreseeable future.

Board members should understand that the selection process involves considerable planning, committed leadership, appropriate financial resources, thoroughness, and flexibility. Without these, the board runs the risk of choosing the wrong person for the job, which could not only be costly but also might cause significant damage to the organization.

PRELIMINARY STEPS

Many boards consider the selection of a special *ad hoc* search committee to be the first step toward selecting a new executive director. However, before that committee is formed, the board should take some key preliminary steps to help ensure that the group will be able to function effectively.

The board should clearly define the mission of the search committee and decide whether it wants the committee to conduct a search on its own or to utilize an executive recruiting firm (or "headhunter") for the search and initial screening. It should then allocate sufficient personnel and financial resources to enable the committee to do a professional job.

The relationship between the board and its search committee can take two forms. One option is for the search committee to bring several top candidates to the attention of the board, with the board making the final decision after formally reviewing the applicants' credentials. The second option, and the one used more frequently, calls for the board to delegate search and selection powers to the committee, with the understanding that the board will be heavily involved in the process and will ratify the committee's final selection.

Because executive recruiting firms often have the ability to locate candidates with higher qualifications, including individuals who may not have considered making a move, such firms can be used effectively in the search process. Yet the cost of employing a recruiting firm is a major consideration for a board to weigh. Currently, the typical cost for such service is equivalent to 30 percent of the executive director's first-year salary, plus additional charges to cover recruiting travel expenses.

Whether an executive recruiting firm is or is not utilized, the board needs to provide enough resources to allow the committee to use a secretary part time to support group activities such as developing candidate files, recording committee minutes, scheduling candidate visits, and arranging for meeting space.

If the committee is going to handle the search on its own, it will also need to hire a knowledgeable part-time person to organize advertising, answer routine questions, make national contacts, and so forth. These important activities should not be left to volunteers, because volunteers may be forced by the demands of their own jobs to give these details less attention than they should.

THE SEARCH COMMITTEE

Once the board has decided how it will conduct its search, the board president should appoint the members of the search committee, making sure they represent the various interests on the board. Without a balanced committee, internal board conflict can easily arise.

The chairperson should be selected with particular care, because he or she will become the top "salesperson" for the organization. This individual should not only have sufficient time to volunteer and the requisite leadership experience to direct the search process, but should also have a broad knowledge of the organization's history, its strengths, and weaknesses.

Although board members should compose a significant majority of the committee, it is also advisable to include a few outsiders in the search group. When outsiders are included, however, they must be individuals who have a broad view of the organization and its functions.

Frequently, former board members can bring helpful perspectives. However, those former board members who revel in nostalgia may actually hamper the progress of the committee and even steer it toward safe, unimaginative candidates. The ideal outside search committee member is most likely a person with both operational management experience and strategic planning skills.

If the organization is community based—for instance, a local social service agency rather than a national organization —it is advisable to have on the committee an outsider with significant experience in the organization's field of expertise. Examples include a professor from a nearby university, a recently retired professional with state-of-the-art knowledge, or an executive director from a similar organization in a neighboring city. Typically, search groups find the knowledge and interpersonal networks of such individuals invaluable.

Staff and management personnel are not usually found on search committees (except at universities and in a few other places). But these personnel should be kept informed as the process proceeds. Needless to say, the entire board should be continually updated on search activity progress.

Once these initial issues have been settled, the committee, with or without an executive recruiting firm, must complete seven steps to conduct the search and select the new executive director:

- Set the criteria and qualifications for the position
- Establish salary and benefit ranges for board approval
- Seek qualified candidates
- Screen potential candidates
- Interview candidates and make recommendations to the board
- Negotiate the hiring of the selected candidate
- Facilitate the employment of the candidate

SETTING CRITERIA FOR THE POSITION

Once the committee is formed, its first task is to develop a functional job description for the position. (See Appendix A, page 95, for an example of such a description.) In some instances, the full board may want to be involved in developing the job description, but this is rarely an efficient or desirable approach to the task.

The job description should reflect the specific performance responsibilities of the executive director. These may be tasks for which he or she is directly responsible or ones that may be delegated. A typical starting point is the current job description, which should be reviewed with regard to present and future realities.

However, the committee should avoid the temptation to use the current description "as is" or merely update it superficially. Both the circumstances of the organization and the executive performance demands are likely to have changed since the prior job description was written.

The group should also avoid another very common pitfall—writing a wish list naming everything an executive could do and every positive human trait he or she should possess. In the early stages, most descriptions represent an impossible ideal. The committee should be certain that the description it finally accepts is one that is reasonably realistic.

In developing the job description, the committee should incorporate its vision of what the organization might become. Committee members must be able to define that vision to ensure that the person they ultimately select is a good fit as the organization evolves. Their objective then becomes hiring a pragmatic visionary, not a person who is just interested in "minding the store."

Specifically, the job description should address three areas—knowledge, skill, and behavior. Knowledge is what an executive needs to know about managing people, about working with a nonprofit board, about funding, and the like. The knowledge base required will vary from organization to organization. For example, if a board assumes total responsibility for fund development, the level of knowledge that the candidate needs in this area would be modest.

Skill involves the ability to take policy direction from the board and implement the board's directives. This includes such managerial activities as program evaluation, staff evaluation, and long-range planning. Personal skills are necessary in areas in which the executive director assumes direct responsibility. However, knowledge may be sufficient where the person delegates responsibility. For example, an executive director will certainly need skills in resolving interpersonal conflict, but may only need reasonable knowledge about financial matters that are delegated to a staff financial manager.

The final area addressed in the job description, the behaviors expected of the executive director, is the hardest to describe in terms of what the organization needs. Yet it is extremely important. A highly aggressive person, for example, may be inappropriate for a small-town organization used to quiet evolution, yet be much more welcome in a fast-paced urban setting.

Whatever the specific requirements of the organization, the executive director's knowledge, skills, and behavior all need to be applied effectively to the four basic areas of management—human resource management, strategic planning and implementation, financial management, and operational management. In our experience, the most important ability an executive director needs is the ability to see that the nonprofit's managerial systems are effective and functioning well.

When the top executive fails to meet broad performance responsibilities, it is usually due to a lack of managerial leadership. The executive director does not have to perform all of the leadership functions personally. But he or she does have to play the *enabler* role to make sure that others in the organization collectively perform all necessary managerial functions.

ESTABLISHING SALARY AND BENEFITS

The search committee needs to recommend a salary range and benefit package to the board for its approval. If the organization has not changed executive directors for a long time, committee members and the board may encounter "sticker shock" when reviewing the salaries currently being paid in the field.

As with any talent in short supply, the market for highly qualified executives is extremely competitive. Quality talent is never inexpensive, but the right person quickly and easily pays for himself or herself. Looking for bargains in hiring top management personnel is foolish. The organization should be prepared to pay the market price for top talent, then expect a high level of performance.

Comparative data on salaries can be located in professional publications, such as *Nonprofit Times* or *The Chronicle of Higher Education*, or through national organizations involved in specific fields. For local comparisons, some United Way organizations, trade, and professional groups are helpful sources of information.

The search committee needs latitude for action in determining salary and benefits in order to offer an attractive package to its top candidate.

SEEKING QUALIFIED CANDIDATES

In general, it is better to err on the side of conducting too wide a search rather than one that is too narrow. Because the selection decision is so critical, any reasonable extra investment in screening a larger pool of candidates usually provides an excellent return. It is possible to become overwhelmed by the number and varied backgrounds of the persons applying for the position. Yet if the group considers *quality* as its major criterion when it begins screening applications, the committee almost never stays overwhelmed for long.

To meet high ethical standards and equal opportunity guidelines, the job opening must be widely publicized to all groups from which candidates might emerge. Advertising costs can be considerable if the job opening is listed in national and local papers, professional journals, and trade publications. Consequently, the committee will have to make some trade-offs on which publications to utilize. Another alternative is to send a letter to an appropriate list of qualified people. Obviously, these communications activities require custom-designed materials based upon the full job description.

At this point, the group should also begin talking directly to key contacts. Persons prominent in the field, academics, chairpersons of similar groups that have recently completed a search, journalists, and volunteers could all be contacted. Many of these individuals attend national or regional conferences in the field and can be approached there. However, a phone call is usually the most expeditious way to obtain helpful advice.

The search committee also needs to be aware that potential candidates will have more questions than published information can answer. Consequently, they must establish a system to forward additional information to applicants who request it. This activity typically is handled by the part-time person responsible for search activities. However, if an executive recruiting firm has been employed, it is responsible for this activity.

SCREENING POTENTIAL CANDIDATES

The first step in screening is to eliminate all persons who are clearly unqualified for the position. Our experience with search committees indicates most should expect to discard about 80 percent of all applications immediately. As a matter of courtesy, these applicants should be quickly notified that they are not being considered for the position.

After the pool has been narrowed to several potential candidates, the search committee must conduct a second screening to select the subgroup of applicants having the highest potential. To do this job well, the committee needs to utilize a checklist of job-related criteria (see Appendix B, page 99, for an example of such a list). The outcome of this second step in the screening process should be the development of a short list of persons whom the group wishes to interview.

Committee members should expect to call or write individual candidates to clarify items on their resumes or to ask additional questions. They will also want to get names of references from these persons for use later in the process. A few references may be contacted prior to a visit, if the committee is uncertain about a candidate. However, the more common procedure is to wait until after the visit. Reference checking is a very complex process, but one that, properly done, can yield significant information. (Appendix F on page 117 provides information on checking references.) Well-managed reference checks provide performance clues vital to selection of a top leader.[1]

After these steps have been completed, the committee is ready to choose approximately six candidates for a visit and personal interview. Along with an invitation, each applicant should receive a detailed package providing information on both the organization and the community (see Appendix C, page 105).

INTERVIEWING CANDIDATES

The visit is much more than a time for candidates and the hosts to talk. It also provides an opportunity for the organization's personnel and other key individuals in the community or association to meet the candidates. Unfortunately, search groups too often make the mistake of asking staff and management to evaluate finalists in social settings, for example, at cocktail parties.

Candidate visits should be structured to give people some opportunity to meet the final candidates in a professional setting. Small group meetings, personal interviews, and business luncheons or dinners are all good ways to facilitate interaction. Those who will work directly with the successful candidate should be encouraged to give their reactions to members of the committee following the visits. How such information is channeled will depend upon the system developed by the organization involved.

The full interview process should take at least one day for each candidate, and each finalist should be told that the one or two top finalists will be invited back for an additional visit.

Sample questions for personal interviews and an interview assessment guide are contained in appendixes D and E, pages 107 to 116. During interviews, committee members should pay particular attention to each candidate's skills and motivations and relate them to the organization's climate and culture as well as its functional needs.

After all initial and follow-up visits have been completed and all background information gathered, the committee should provide its list of recommended candidates to the board. If the search group has been entrusted with the mission of selecting the top person, the committee will submit his or her name and a list of second and third choices for the board's consideration.

NEGOTIATING A CONTRACT

After the board has either ratified the committee's selection or chosen the top candidate from a short list supplied by the committee, the board president should immediately contact the selected candidate and make a firm offer of employment. The board needs to allow its president a great deal of negotiating discretion, allowing him or her to modify the offer should the candidate have special requirements.

An attractive candidate can be frustrated if she or he has to wait while the president gets board approval for modest changes involving, for example, the use of a car, health benefits, pension benefits, starting dates, or vacation time.

All verbal agreements made between the board president and the selected candidate need to be put in writing in an employment letter. This letter should specify a starting date and a date by which the offer must be accepted or rejected. All relevant details and understandings should be included. Omitting even some small items can cause problems later.

FACILITATING EMPLOYMENT

After an employment agreement has been reached, all of the unsuccessful final candidates should be notified promptly and thanked for their interest. A press release should be written, and plans for the transition established (see chapter 3). If the announcement warrants a press conference as well as a press release, the conference should be held when the candidate can be present. This is also a time when transitional talks can begin between the candidate and his or her predecessor, particularly if they have had little previous opportunity to communicate extensively.

The committee should save all records of its activities, not only for reference in future searches but also as data in the event that equal employment opportunity issues are raised at any time by a governmental agency.

THE UNTHINKABLE—REOPENING THE SEARCH

Occasionally search groups fail to find an acceptable candidate or none of the finalists accepts the position offered. As disagreeable as it may be to consider reopening the search, the committee may confront that possibility. The group needs to know when to consider reopening the search, how much of the process it needs to repeat, and what it needs to change in its procedures.

In making a reassessment, the members should review why the finalists rejected the position and also determine why all those who applied seemed unacceptable to the committee. The reasons may have nothing to do with the organization or its search process—the top candidate may have accepted another job offer or found his or her spouse reluctant to move —or they may relate directly to the position itself.

If the latter is true, the committee will have to consider redefining the position, recommending a different compensation package, or both. In reviewing the qualifications and criteria for the position, the committee and the full board will have to assess which duties are absolutely vital and which might be delegated to other staff or to board members. Candidates must see the job as challenging but also as doable. In addition, the total compensation package must be commensurate with the demands of the job.

Should a second search be unavoidable, the board and search group should ask themselves the following questions.

- How well did our job description fit the candidate pool?
- How effective were the methods we used for developing the pool of candidates?
- Was the interview process handled with adequate dispatch and sophistication?
- Were expectations on both sides explicitly defined and agreed upon?
- Did the top candidates have a good feeling about the way in which the search was completed?
- Did the search process really focus on relevant performance issues rather than only on questions of personality and public image?
- Did all rejected candidates have a positive feeling about their experiences in the selection process?
- Are those candidates who were rejected likely to think favorably about the organization in the future?

The discussion around each of these questions will help all involved to decide what needs to be done differently during the second search.

NOTES

Some information in this chapter and related appendixes has been drawn from *Executive Selection in Family Service Agencies* (Milwaukee, WI: Family Service America, 1986).

1. Thomas N. Gilmore, *Making a Leadership Change* (San Francisco: Jossey-Bass, 1988), pp. 82–87.

3

CUSTOM DESIGN YOUR NEW EXECUTIVE'S ORIENTATION PROGRAM

The long and time-consuming executive selection process is finally over, and the new executive director is eager to begin. Board members, particularly those who served on the search committee, are ready to let the nonprofit's new director take charge.

But the board's job is only partially finished. Board members have a key obligation to ensure an effective and efficient transfer of operational responsibility from the former executive to the new one. Hiring the right person for the job is step one. The second, and equally important, step is to get the new executive off to a solid start.

An effective orientation program, tailored to the needs of the new executive, is essential. The length of the orientation program will vary depending upon the situation, but in all instances should be completed within the new executive's first year. Such a program is a key element in any leadership change. This program is especially important when the new executive is succeeding an incumbent who has resigned under board pressure.

Properly designed and implemented, the orientation program ensures that top management responsibility is transferred smoothly, without undue disruption for the organization and its members or clients.

BOARD ALTERNATIVES

Typically, a nonprofit board will approach the task of getting the new executive "on board" in one of three different ways. The first two approaches are successful in certain situations, but the third approach is preferable in the majority of cases.

COMPLETE DELEGATION

The first approach is for the board quickly and completely to delegate all management responsibility to the new executive. In this "complete delegation" scenario, the board asks its new executive to work on goals and objectives within weeks of the time he or she takes office. Total time for orientation rarely exceeds two months when the board uses this approach.

This short-term orientation strategy works well only when the new executive director is being promoted from within the organization or by chance has a significant strategic understanding of the organization. In either event, the new executive must have both an acknowledged track record and a superior understanding of the organization's climate for the strategy to work.

PUBLIC RELATIONS AND EARLY DELEGATION

The second board approach is similar to the first, with one significant difference. The board recognizes that its new director needs exposure in the local community. Perhaps he or she has come from another area and is unknown by the community or has been involved in another organization in the area that has a very different constituency.

In this second scenario, the board carefully orchestrates a social and public relations program for its new executive to maximize the impact it desires to achieve in the wider community or industry. At the same time, the board gives the exec-

29

utive the go-ahead for the complete and early development of the nonprofit's goals and objectives.

The "public relations/early delegation" approach tends to work best when the new executive is recognized as a "pro" and is also reasonably familiar with the organization and its internal and external climates. In such cases, the orientation program can usually be completed within a three- to four-month period.

THE CUSTOM-DESIGNED ORIENTATION

The third approach requires a longer time frame for full implementation, but does more to meet the needs of the majority of new executives and nonprofit boards. In this scenario, a board committee structures a formal orientation program with the active participation of its new executive. The custom-designed program is tailored to the individual and the specific nonprofit group. Such a program helps the new executive develop a solid base in the organization and understand its unique climate and culture. It also ties the incoming executive to the nonprofit's operating environment.

Properly structured, this type of orientation program takes approximately one year to complete. Time commitment on the part of the board decreases over the course of the year. Responsibility for the success of the program should be shouldered by one or more senior board members. Whenever possible, it is desirable to have the volunteer president or chairperson accept the responsibility for program completion.

The most successful orientation programs of this type involve weekly or biweekly meetings between the senior board member(s) and the new executive director. However, both sides should be wary if the amount of contact time between the two does not decrease considerably as the year progresses. If this does not happen, an unhealthy managerial dependency on the board often occurs. On the other hand, if the executive and board members do not meet regularly, an equally unhealthy "expectation gap" develops. Because communication is spotty, neither knows what the other expects. Such a gap can lead to undesirable board involvement in the operations of the organization. In these situations, the board can unintentionally become overinvolved in management-level decisions.

With this scenario, the board must take care to delegate responsibility properly. Boards that *overdelegate* give their new executive too much responsibility too quickly. Those that *underdelegate* don't give the executive the necessary power and authority to meet objectives. Also of concern are *vague and inconsistent delegation.* Vague delegation leaves too many areas that are gray or imprecise. Inconsistent delegation leaves the new executive uncertain about boundaries and backing.

Every custom-designed orientation program should include eight steps. Some must be taken in sequence, others can proceed concurrently. Let the specific situation determine the guidelines. The eight steps are:

1. Developing immediate and long-term goals
2. Reviewing fiscal and personnel resources
3. Examining current policies and procedures
4. Developing staff relationships
5. Fostering board relationships
6. Cultivating community or industry associations
7. Understanding the clientele or membership
8. Discussing the new executive's career expectations

Developing Immediate and Long-Term Goals: In the first few weeks, the new executive director and the board member or members responsible for the transition program need to agree on immediate, short-term operational or tactical goals. These goals involve current issues requiring quick resolution. They usually spring from unresolved operational issues left over from the previous administration.

Working together with the board on these problems helps the new director get a feel for the climate and pressures under which such decisions are currently being made. It also gives the new executive a quick overview of the historical basis for current concerns, plus a feel for the strategic thinking of the board. In addition, it facilitates the development of a formal communications channel and interpersonal rapport between the executive and the board.

Establishing more formal long term-goals should wait until the new person has been on the job for four to six months and has had time fully to assess the nonprofit's situation. It is wise to wait because these long-term goals should be used later as the basis for evaluating the executive's performance.

Such a waiting period gives the newcomer sufficient time to evaluate personnel and resources. It will also give him or her an opportunity to get to know board members and their expectations.

When the long-term goals are developed, the initial draft should be written by the executive director. This not only insures "ownership" of the proposed goals but also allows the executive to begin a comparative strategic thinking process. For example, the executive must consider the nonprofit's role in the community or industry along with its marketing plan for providing appropriate customer or client services. Resource bases and "customer service" perceptions are also important for the executive to look at in a strategic context.

Development of the final goals will almost always involve additional drafts and alterations. The objective is to set goals that move the organization forward and also have the significant support of the board and the executive. In situations in which individual board members have distinctly different priorities and goals, the astute executive will work to gain overall board commitment to a single plan.

Reviewing Fiscal and Personnel Resources: During the hiring process, candidates for the top executive position should have asked for and been given a broad overview of the nonprofit's fiscal and personnel resources. At the time the executive begins the job, however, he or she needs to have a financial review by the organization's external auditors, unless such a review has recently been completed.

The auditors should be asked to make special note of any unusual transactions that have taken place since the previous external audit. Subsequently, all items in the auditor's management letter should be reviewed by the board and the new executive so that all are in agreement on items requiring policy and operational action.

The new executive director and the senior board member responsible for the executive's transition also need to seek the views of the external auditors regarding the capabilities of incumbent financial personnel.

In conducting the personnel-resources review, the executive should consider current job assignments as they relate to individual employee skills and motivations. In other words, he or she should determine the "person–job" fit for all positions.

33

Simultaneously, the executive can discuss with individual board members their views of the current level of organizational performance and effectiveness.

After approximately six months on the job, the executive should arrange a short human-resources review with key board members. The purpose of the review is to develop board understanding about staff strengths and weaknesses in relation to mission and tasks. In addition, this meeting gives the board insight on needed organizational or staff changes.

This total assessment of the strengths and weaknesses of financial and personnel resources should be completed by the executive in his or her first six months on the job.

Examining Current Policies and Procedures: Reviewing policies and procedures is a routine but necessary task. The top administrative staff should be responsible for the executive's orientation on operating policies and procedures.

The executive will also develop a fuller understanding of such policies and procedures as he or she makes daily operating decisions.

However, when it comes to understanding how the board goes about setting policy, the executive needs a formal "tutorial" orientation. Because the board president or chairperson is the individual most likely to have broad background information on board policies and procedures, the board's leader should take responsibility for this activity.

Whether at the administrative or the board level, all of the nonprofit's policies and procedures should be simple, understandable, and operationally complete. The executive and the senior board member in charge of orientation should establish a work plan to determine if the organization's policies and procedures meet these criteria. The task can be simple or extensive, depending upon the quality of prior work. Any board member asked to work with the new executive on this task will need to be thoroughly familiar with the status and background history of key board policies and procedures.

Developing Staff Relationships: In any organization, top management changes cause staff insecurity and unrest. With a new operating chief, it is reasonable to expect that the organizational structure will be modified and that jobs will be deleted, added, or rearranged. Inevitably, the new structure will require changes in interpersonal and work relationships. Old, comfortable patterns will be broken. Resistance to change will likely occur.

The new executive must quickly become a "transformational leader," that is, a person capable of leading the organization through change.[1] In individual and group meetings, and in countless other ways, the executive must take responsibility for responding to employee concerns.

The board's responsibility, in turn, is to support its new executive in this task. Board members must provide strong support for changes that are needed. The board can also assist the director in other ways, for example, by sponsoring informal social events to allow board members to communicate directly with staff about the changes. The board should also be aware of the need to have strong board representation at all business meetings or functions where the board is traditionally expected to participate. In other words, the board should strongly support the new executive and the changes he or she is making.

Fostering Board Relationships: Any politically astute new executive will want to get to know his or her board well, and board members should expect a strong leader assertively to develop these interpersonal relationships. One practical sugges-

35

tion is for the new executive to meet initially with individual board members at their place of employment or another convenient location. If the executive does not make such a proposal, the board should suggest it. Informal breakfast or luncheon meetings also can be helpful when the executive wants to present new ideas informally to individual board members.

Cultivating Community or Industry Associations: The board president or chairperson needs to assume strong leadership in helping the new executive develop contacts and relationships, both with other board members and with community or industry leaders. This is particularly important when the organization is a trade or professional group, but it is useful for a new executive in just about any organization. Networking opportunities can take many forms, including formal social receptions for the newcomer, introductions to various members of the media, or invitations to functions attended by community and industry leaders. The board should encourage its new executive to seek as much public exposure as possible, through speaking engagements, news releases, or by other means. Being well known in the community or industry is especially beneficial for the executive who needs to be involved in fund raising.

Boards should have an actual game plan to help their new executive become integrated in the community or industry. The plan should be developed jointly by the board and the new executive and followed conscientiously.

Understanding the Clientele or Membership: Tactics useful in developing board or community relationships also apply to clients and members. Through informal meetings, presentations, or reviews of pertinent issues, the board should strive to give its new executive an understanding of how the services provided by the organization are perceived by clients, members, and other external constituencies. In the words of Tom Peters and Bob Waterman, internationally known management experts, the board needs to encourage the executive director to "get close to the customer."[2]

Discussing the New Executive's Career Expectations: When the board hires a new executive director, it should have an understanding of that individual's career expectations and aspirations and be certain that these expectations are compatible with the executive's new position.[3] The board and the new director must agree on a plan for career development and growth, and the board should specify what it is willing to do to help the director along that path.

The board should consider the executive's professional development a necessary investment in the organization's survival and growth. It is true that many executives who develop professionally eventually leave for better-paying jobs elsewhere. Yet it is also true that nonprofit organizations that insist on and assist in top management development tend to retain better-performing executive directors. Organizations that don't encourage professional development tend to employ "compliant mediocrities."

BENEFITS OF A CUSTOM-DESIGNED APPROACH TO ORIENTATION

Numerous benefits accrue to having a board-directed orientation program for a new executive director. The most important is the smooth transition that such a program promotes. Power, authority, leadership, and accountability are clearly understood and accepted by both the board and its new director. Conflict is reduced.

Joint board–director problem solving helps not only the new executive but also the entire organization to start off on the right foot. In effect, what the board and executive negotiate, through completion of a custom-designed orientation program, is a "psychological contract." The term "psychological contract," coined by behavioral analysts Victor Vroom and Harry Levinson, means that both board and director have a clear and mutual understanding of goals, priorities, and delegation boundaries.[4]

In turn, effective delegation gives the board necessary policy control and direction. It also gives the new executive operational authority to obtain high-performance output from the organization.

The board that meets its obligation formally to orient a new executive director can expect to have a smoother-running organization and to enjoy community support and approval. The board will also be free to perform its most important functions—development and monitoring of policy and visionary planning.

NOTES

1. Noel Tichy and Mary Anne Devanna, *The Transformational Leader* (New York: John Wiley and Sons, 1986).

2. Thomas Peters and Robert Waterman, *In Search of Excellence* (New York: Harper and Row, 1982), p. 156.

3. Edgar Schein, "Increasing Organizational Effectiveness through Better Human Resource Planning and Development," in *Readings in Human Resource Management,* edited by Michael Beer and Bert Spector (New York: The Free Press, 1985). See page 382 for an individual-needs model for human resource planning and development.

4. Edgar Schein, *Organizational Psychology* (Englewood Cliffs, NJ: Prentice-Hall, 1972).

4

THE EFFECTIVE EXECUTIVE TAKES OVER

After six months in his new position as executive director of the not-for-profit XYZ Agency, Hal Cordy took time out to assess his own performance. Had he done everything possible to assume responsibility for his new organization?

From his desk drawer, Hal pulled out the plan he had developed prior to taking the position, the third, and probably last, major move in his 30-year career. The nonprofit organization he had recently joined was very similar in objectives and character to the two he had previously managed. Hal, however, was well aware that successful nonprofit management is highly situational.[1] The working culture and the interpersonal relationships in every organization give each its own unique dimensions.

ASSESSING CRITICAL RESOURCES

Hal's first objective had been to get an organizational "feel" for his new situation. He did this by making quick, preliminary judgments in four major areas: financial resources, staff competence, group commitment, and organizational climate.

FINANCIAL RESOURCES

Prior to assuming his new responsibilities, Hal had received the organization's operating statements and management letters for the previous two years. His new organization appeared to be stable from a financial standpoint. Yet, Hal knew, financial statements can sometimes conceal serious problems.

For that reason, Hal's plan had called for an in-depth review of finances with his new financial officer and the external auditors. He had also made an appointment to visit with the loan officer at the bank that had extended the organization a line of credit.

His discussions with the external auditors and the bank official had a dual purpose. He wanted their assessment of the nonprofit's financial condition. He also wanted their private assessment of how competent they found the organization's financial personnel to be. Hal had only a general background in financial areas. He felt his financial staff had to have superior skills if he was to be successful in his own job. The future held enough challenges. Hal didn't want to lie awake at night wondering whether the financial side of the organization was adequately handled.

Early in his tenure, Hal had also taken time to get to know his board's finance committee members. From experience he knew that the members of this group could not—and should not—shoulder any detailed financial responsibility. Yet finance committee members could be very valuable in communicating financial information to the whole board.

After the initial round of meetings and review sessions had been completed, Hal decided he had no reason to make major changes in the organization's financial operations or personnel. However, he wasn't sorry for the time spent in assessing the situation. He had needed to assure himself that all financial matters were in good hands. If they weren't, he would have been in a position to make changes quickly.

Hal was relieved to know that he was not faced with financial surprises that might force him to reorganize quickly or lay off staff—typically the only options for "people-intensive" nonprofit organizations in financial crisis. He realized that such a predicament would be less than ideal for a new executive director.

STAFF COMPETENCE

From experience, Hal knew that staff competence is a critical issue for any nonprofit organization. Full organizational productivity cannot be achieved unless staff members have the requisite level of competence. However, the long-term potential of some staff members is difficult to assess. This is especially true in organizations composed largely of individual contributors who interact with clients or members on a one-to-one basis.

In evaluating several key persons in his previous post, it had taken Hal some time to distinguish between those who were mired in sincere but ineffective short-term activity and those who were oriented to accomplishing long-term organizational goals. In drafting his action plan for XYZ, Hal was determined to minimize the time required to get an accurate and objective "performance fix" on key personnel.

In keeping with that plan, Hal had reviewed all the available personnel and performance records to determine the level of productivity achieved by key staff. He had also personally interviewed key personnel. After those interviews were completed, he discussed the "performance perceptions" of those staff members with their superiors.

For those individuals reporting directly to him, Hal turned to his predecessor for counsel. He knew such an approach had its limitations. People respond to various leadership styles and management motivations differently. An employee might be productive under one manager and yet fail to grow and develop under another. However, Hal reasoned, most people develop a performance track record over time. Mediocre performers seldom become high performers. Likewise, high performers seldom drastically reduce their professional efforts.

Hal's stated goal was to distinguish between the more effective organizational producers and their sincere, but ineffective, associates. Any delays or miscalculations in achieving this goal would be detrimental to moving the organization forward. Long-range planning, his action plan noted, would also be hampered because it depended upon the efforts of a competent staff.

GROUP COMMITMENT

Hal's new organization had a strategic plan in place. It was based on his predecessor's vision of the organization's strengths and opportunities. Hal's action plan called for assessing the commitment of staff and board members to the goals delineated by that strategic plan.

To get that assessment, he asked the board to form a committee composed of board and staff members. The committee was asked to evaluate the strategic plan and suggest a process for its review and revision. He considered the project important, but not as crucial as his assessment of financial operations and staff competence. Consequently, he asked the group to complete its work in approximately six months.

43

To show that he was genuinely interested in the planning process, Hal assumed the job of chairing the committee. One of his managers accepted responsibility for getting the necessary staff work completed. To give himself a greater understanding of the organization's interpersonal situation, Hal had named staff persons with differing levels of experience and tenure as committee members. He had also asked the board chairperson to use the same criteria for selecting the three board representatives on the committee.

Hal's action plan noted that his overall objective was to determine whether the strategic plan was viable and workable. Throughout his career, he had observed a number of instances in which the strategic plan was a useless "shelf" document, without any tangible impact on the organization.

A secondary objective was to ascertain which persons were primarily committed to the stated aims of the organization and which to more self-serving or specialized agendas. He knew that his committee's work to evaluate the plan would give him the perspective he needed on the commitments of the various interest groups in the organization.

Hal wanted these personal insights because he knew that nonprofit groups are sometimes structured to meet the needs of the management and staff rather than the needs of the clients or members. He wanted to promote a client-centered—not an employee-centered—approach for the organization.

ORGANIZATIONAL CLIMATE

During the interview process, Hal felt comfortable with XYZ's board and staff. They seemed open to questions and willing to discuss not only XYZ's strengths and opportunities but also the issues and difficulties that would affect its future.

His initial impression was that the staff worked well together and that the level of political conflict within the organization was reasonable. However, his action plan noted the need for some immediate steps to determine whether his first impressions were correct. Otherwise it might be some time before he could get a reading on the organizational climate. The cordial "honeymoon period" experienced by most new senior executives often makes it difficult to get an objective analysis of the situation. Harmony and optimism are the norm. Few staff persons want to bring conflicting or negative news to their new executive director.

In his first months on the job, Hal not only took advantage of every formal and informal contact to help monitor key facets of the organizational climate but also hosted a series of late-afternoon coffee hours in the staff lounge.

Specific individuals from various parts of the organization were invited to each coffee hour, and the group attending each was deliberately kept small. To make people comfortable, Hal had allowed time for informal discussion of personal topics, including hobbies, vacations, and travel plans. Next he turned to the operations of the organization, and allowed conversation to range widely. After the first few coffee hours, the "grapevine" spread the word that Hal was sincerely interested in getting positive as well as negative feedback. The sessions, furthermore, helped Hal determine which of his initial impressions of the organization's climate had been accurate.

BECOMING A LEADER

Most of Hal's first three months on the job were taken up with assessment actions. The second three-month period, according to his plan, was to be devoted to building upon what he had learned and to taking steps to establish his leadership role.

Hal glanced at the action plan on his desk and noted that he had given himself five specific goals:

- Establish his role as a transformational leader
- Determine managerial risks that needed to be assumed
- Fill gaps in the administrative system
- Develop community or industry relationships
- Develop a leadership posture with respect to his board and his predecessor

TRANSFORMATIONAL LEADER

Hal's plan underscored the need to establish his role as a leader who would bring about change and possibly alter the organization's direction. Any major change in leadership brings feelings of uncertainty and insecurity, even to the most productive staff in an organization. Consequently, Hal took every opportunity to talk informally with the staff and the board about new initiatives and challenges.

He sought to establish a theme or statement around which the staff and board could identify his administration. Such a statement is not unlike those developed by political leaders to clarify their aims, such as Lyndon Johnson's "Great Society" or George Bush's "kinder and gentler" America. Hal's predecessor had developed such a theme, and Hal decided after a discussion with several people that it was a good one that only needed to be modified.

Hal had also made an effort to let others who were looking for positive change know that he sought their support. He had asked the staff to give him their ideas for improvements in brief written form. He responded to each suggestion verbally, letting the person know what he thought was currently viable and what might receive future consideration. Where possible, he incorporated staff recommendations into his program and always gave full credit to the person making the suggestion.

Hal felt that all of these actions would set the stage for his being viewed as a transformational leader. He managed each of the activities personally. Consequently, he informally monitored results through the comments and perceptions of others in the organization.

MANAGERIAL RISKS

To keep the organization moving in a positive direction, Hal prioritized new and existing programs on a cost–benefit basis. He also developed a list of priorities that reflected his own tolerance for taking risks. Items on the top of his list reflected areas in which he was most willing to take risks. These areas would receive more of his attention than would items further down the list. To be certain that the board agreed with his priorities, he had asked for and received its formal endorsement of his priorities.

Hal also looked for small problems or organizational glitches that needed to be addressed quickly. Correcting minor but annoying problems in systems or programs involved little risk but sent a strong signal to the staff that the new executive director was alert to long-standing problems and headaches.

ADMINISTRATIVE GAPS

Hal's 30 years of experience as a professional manager had taught him that any large or medium-sized nonprofit organization has administrative problems that need to be resolved. Organizations develop habits and traditions that can be counterproductive. Hal had observed over the years that staff could sometimes confuse "just doing things" with productive activity.

Hal made a point of looking for opportunities to reduce bureaucratic inertia or poor performance. He had, for example, perceived that he could increase production in several departments by spending a little money on high-speed computer printers. The purchases were authorized and the printers were in use within a week. That step was only one of several he made. Each had some immediate, observable impact on the organization's performance and staff motivation. Such actions, Hal realized now, also supported his goal of being a transformational leader.

COMMUNITY RELATIONSHIPS

With the assistance of the board chairperson, Hal developed a two-step program to introduce himself to local community and business leaders.

The first step was a late-afternoon reception at a local hotel, hosted by the board for Hal and his wife, to which XYZ board members and community leaders were invited. The board chairperson made welcoming remarks, and Hal responded in what appeared to be an informal manner. In reality, his response had been well developed and rehearsed.

The next step was a letter from the board chairperson to industrial leaders telling of Hal's appointment. The letter indicated that the chairperson would appreciate the recipient meeting with Hal for a few minutes to get acquainted. Hal followed up by making appointments to see individuals who had received the letter.

Both activities brought Hal a base of community and professional contacts that he could use to promote the interests of the organization.

48

DEALING WITH PAST AND CURRENT LEADERSHIP

To build communication and understanding, Hal and the board chairperson decided to meet informally every 10 days or so during Hal's first three months. Hal found the meetings helpful in making operational decisions that were in keeping with board policies. The discussions also helped him get a better understanding of how the board operated and how various members related to one another.

The informal discussions also helped Hal and his board chairperson determine just how much support Hal needed from the board. When a strong new executive director takes over, it is not unusual for the board to relax and delegate too much responsibility. Too often, executive directors in such organizations are thus denied the reasonable support they need to get their programs going.

Hal and the board chairperson ended their informal meetings according to their deadline, because they agreed that continuing to meet might promote too much board involvement in day-to-day activities.

On the other hand, Hal continued to have occasional meetings with his predecessor, who had remained in the area. His predecessor had been with the organization for a long time, and both Hal and the former executive thought occasional meetings would be helpful.

DID HAL'S LEADERSHIP PLAN WORK?

After reviewing his activities for the past six months, Hal concluded that his plan for becoming an effective executive director of his new organization had been successful. The plan included nine specific areas. He had covered all of the areas but had given priority to the first four: assessing financial resources, staff competence, group commitment, and organizational climate.

He felt comfortable that he was applying sound transformational leadership techniques to improve the organization's performance and climate. He also felt he had prioritized managerial risks, filled gaps in the administrative system, developed professional and community relationships, and marshalled appropriate support from both his board and his predecessor.

ASSUMING LEADERSHIP OF AN ORGANIZATION IN TROUBLE

A year later, a friend of Hal's came to him with concerns about a job he'd been offered. The friend had been asked to become the new executive director of a nonprofit organization that had some serious problems.

Hal offered his friend a copy of both his leadership plan and his extensive notes, which he'd made in his first six months on the job. After reviewing the information, the friend asked Hal to indicate the changes he would make in his leadership plan if he were to become the executive director of an organization in serious difficulty.

Hal offered the following suggestions:

■ **Obtain a new external financial audit or an update of the most recent external audit.** This provides a current assessment of how fiscal controls are operating and highlights important financial concerns.

■ **Meet monthly with the board finance committee.** They should have a good understanding of the financial situation. In addition, they can provide support if quick fiscal changes must take place.

■ **Ask a trusted consultant to provide an objective, third-party evaluation of key personnel.** This will help provide a rationale for any personnel changes that need to be made quickly. It should also help the executive director assess staff strengths and weaknesses more quickly.

■ **Establish a board–staff committee composed of individuals with reputations for being creative thinkers and doers.** Ask for their suggestions for increasing revenues, enhancing fundraising efforts, and cutting costs. Have key committee members work with you to implement needed changes.

■ **Make decisions quickly and limit participation in decision making to a reasonable level of staff involvement.** Don't let matters drag for too long. Be alert to persons or groups who want to prolong the discussion process either to further their own private agendas or because they have inadequate skills.

■ **Make necessary administrative changes as quickly as possible.** Don't hesitate to move quickly to remedy long-standing administrative problems. The high-performance group of staff members will be delighted, and low achievers may see the handwriting on the wall and plan their departures.

NOTE

1. Paul Hersey and Kenneth Blanchard, *Management of Organizational Behavior* (Englewood Cliffs, NJ: Prentice Hall, 1982).

5

MANAGING DIFFERENT TYPES OF EMPLOYEE GROUPS

Executive directors in large, well-established nonprofit organizations tend to think of the professionals on their staff as individual contributors. These individuals are persons who mainly work on their own and not as team players—for instance, counselors, health care professionals, or curators. Many executive directors, however, fail to recognize that these individual contributors often can be grouped according to identifiable employee types, and each group needs to be managed differently.

One group yearns for the "good old days" and is unresponsive to the need for critical changes. Another is adverse to taking risks or giving extra effort because it is comfortable with current operations. Another supports changes that enable professionals to work more efficiently as individuals. Still another group has a commitment to build the organization.

From years of observation of a variety of nonprofits, we have identified four major groups of employees, which we label "Nostalgics," "Maintainers," "Producers," and "Builders." Executive directors who do not recognize the existence of such groups and the special need to manage them differently may not achieve the forward motion or the performance goals they seek in their own organizations.

The executive director needs to understand that professionals in each group typically share common attitudes, perceptions, and value systems. Most important is the fact that each group has its own distinctive responses to organizational performance requirements and rewards. One group's response differs dramatically from another's. In fact, informal group working values—not formal management expectations—tend to determine much of what will be accomplished within an organization.[1]

It is the long-term human resources task of the executive director to encourage those groups of employees who want to improve the nonprofit and to reduce the influence of those who want to maintain a modest performance level.[2] A politically active reactionary group can pressure high-performance individual contributors to the detriment of the whole organization in several ways, ranging from casual admonition through strong negative pressure and ostracism.[3]

An identifiable group may dominate a department or it may have members in different departments. In many cases, a single group may include people with very disparate personalities but whose work-value systems are similar.

Meet, for example, Sarah Thomas, a congenial department head who has spent the past decade in a nonprofit trade association, and Jack Engels, a brusque cost accountant in the association's financial division. Sarah is well liked by the members of her department, while Jack is largely left alone in his work.

On the surface, Sarah and Jack appear to have little in common. Closer observation, however, shows that they are alike in one important respect. Sarah's department, which she has headed for the past six years, performs at a satisfactory but not outstanding level. Over the years, Sarah has tended to hire professionals for her staff who have values like her own. They are good—but not outstanding—performers who support the status quo. The group gets its regular work done but rarely puts forth any extra effort. A recurring complaint from Sarah and her people is that "the department has too much to do."

Consequently, Sarah and her staff always question new programs and changes in terms of how much extra work will be involved. They ask whether enough planning has been accomplished to support the change and whether the new initiatives will stretch the people in the organization too far. Other managers have come to realize that Sarah and her staff are opposed to taking risks and don't embrace new methods or generate creative ideas. For that reason, some of Sarah's peers view her as largely oriented to maintaining the status quo.

Jack Engels, who is never described as congenial by his co-workers, also gets his work done, even though he shows little enthusiasm for what he's doing. He views his work as a job, and is adverse to coming in five minutes early or leaving half an hour after his normal quitting time. He is technically competent but also reluctant to consider new methods. He views increased productivity expectations as unfair pressures and an intrusion on his comfortable professional and personal life.

Both Sarah and Jack are Maintainers, for both are comfortable with the status quo. If the executive director in Sarah's and Jack's nonprofit organization were to allow their group's standards to dominate overall performance standards, the organization would likely stagnate and eventually decline.

The performance-minded executive director needs to understand how the work value systems of various groups of employees have formed over time. He or she must also investigate the links among values, expectations, and life-styles of the various groups, in order to determine how each group relates to the others.[4]

The executive director must not only know how to motivate the various groups but also how to balance them properly. Without a proper balance of group values, organizational conflict is likely to develop. The executive director's only answer to such conflict would be to favor the values of one group outwardly at the expense of the other three, because the groups look at the place of work in their lives so differently. Such a response could lead to either desirable or undesirable results, depending on how it affects organizational productivity.

However, if an executive director is able to motivate and balance the individual contributor groups and their outputs, the result should guarantee a high level of organizational performance.

NOSTALGICS

Nostalgics are generally easy to recognize because they identify so strongly with the organization's past history and culture. Many of them tend to be long-term employees whose performance has leveled off over time.

By and large, they are willing workers who don't mind extra duty on weekends or occasional evening assignments. They take pride in being "company people."

Yet, because of their ties to the past, Nostalgics are uncomfortable with changes they perceive as breaking sharply with tradition. They are likely, for example, to subtly resist efforts to expand computer operations within their organization.

Typically, they also resent changes designed to improve group and individual task performance. Such changes are usually greeted with fear, eliciting statements that the organization to which they have so long given their loyalty is becoming "cold and uncaring." One often hears a Nostalgic say, "I never thought I would see the day when this organization would do something like this."

To properly motivate Nostalgics, the nonprofit director needs to honor and recognize ceremonially special emotional landmarks. Past achievements, the memory of valued associates, key holidays, birthdays, and so forth should be warmly celebrated by top management. In addition, the executive director should sincerely convey to Nostalgics the message that "if it weren't for your contributions, our organization would not be where it is today."

To enhance future growth within the organization, the executive director must show this group how a proposed change will perpetuate the past by building a secure long-term organizational future. In a social work agency, for example, the director could reaffirm the organization's basic tenets of established clinical practice and indicate that any changes would take place slowly and receive thorough evaluation prior to implementation.

To sum up, the following strategies are helpful in dealing with Nostalgics:

- Respond to their need to revere and emotionally relive the past
- Encourage the "willing worker" value system of group members
- Show how proposed changes will perpetuate past glory by contributing to organizational longevity and prominence
- Recognize that Nostalgics lack vision and prefer to avoid direct confrontation about the future direction of the organization

MAINTAINERS

The largest group in virtually all organizations is composed of Maintainers. As illustrated by Jack and Sarah, they are average performers who typically have less tenure but also possess more currently useful skills than Nostalgics.

Maintainers are professionals who think and act like members of a large industrial union. Like union employees who "work to scale" or do only what is required by written contract, Maintainers see increased productivity expectations as an imposition on their comfortable life-styles.

Typically, many of their major life satisfactions are obtained outside of their professional activities. Although they appreciate having a professional position, they have not internally accepted the self-directed performance behavior one typically associates with being a professional.

Unlike the Nostalgic, the Maintainer is not willing to do something extra when the organization needs it. Maintainers usually accomplish most of what is needed by performing at a minimal or average level. Asking them to perform more professionally and to meet higher organizational performance standards frequently triggers resentful, hostile reactions. When major performance changes seem imminent, they quickly coalesce into a defensive political clique.

The more moderate Maintainers seek exemption from higher standards of conduct and performance by requesting the employee's equivalent of "grandfather clauses." They argue that "this wasn't a part of expectations when we were hired." In their view, being able to move from average to slightly above average performance is a significant improvement in level of achievement.

More hostile, active, and vocal Maintainers will become group leaders whenever a new executive director attempts to improve organizational performance standards, especially if the improvement affects their personal or professional life-styles. Although they are usually marginal-to-average producers in their own right, these Maintainers develop political alliances with others who may have long-term performance difficulties. In the long run, hostile Maintainers become apologists or protectors for the inept people in the organization. Such political alliances can be highly detrimental to the organization.[5]

When a new executive director is hired, Maintainers work hard to ensure the new person will either be of marginal or modest ability—so higher performance standards will not be set—or be an individual whose perceived limitations and "average" track record will give Maintainers hope that they can influence the director's key performance decisions through the use of intimidation.[6]

In a political confrontation with a new executive director, Maintainers are sometimes willing to see the nonprofit organization unionized in order to protect their own group's limited performance values. To maintain the status quo, they use the organizational grapevine to arouse defensive anxieties among the Nostalgics.

Failure to deal effectively with Maintainers leads to both prolonged internal skirmishes and to intergroup vendettas. Such dysfunctional behaviors, in turn, drain individual and organizational energy that could be used for constructive change.

Several guidelines are helpful in working with Maintainers:
- Be alert to the strong "union" value system at work in this professional group.

- Depend on group members for low to average productivity but be aware that requests for increased productivity or increased self-management are likely to generate resentment and hostility.
- Emphasize the pressures in the organization's external environment that require professional performance improvement. Indicate how such improvements are important to long-term job security.
- Set modest but attainable performance-improvement goals on an annual basis. (Note: If a complete turnaround is essential for organizational survival, this slow improvement pace will not be adequate.)
- Expect some continuing hostility whenever Maintainers feel new standards put pressure on them for sustained higher performance and commitment.

Because many Maintainers confuse activity with output, they equate being busy with making an organizational contribution. They may never be able to become fully self-managing professionals. As Peter Drucker, the world-renowned management expert, says, "One can expect adults to develop manners and behavior and to learn skills and knowledge. But one has to use people's personalities the way they are, not the way we would like them to be."[7] Similarly, we believe that the effective executive also has to use people's *work values* the way they are, not the way one would like them to be, to manage and motivate employees effectively.

PRODUCERS

Producers are not a clearly defined subgroup in the non-profit organization. In fact, they are not a group in the classic sense but rather a collection of highly individual "type-A workaholics" who are motivated by their own goals.

They tend to work on their own and dislike group activities intensely. Because work output is the core of their existence, they see few differences between their personal and professional lives. They only coalesce as a group when they perceive threats to their performance-oriented life-styles. To the extent that they value and continually produce strong efforts and a high level of output, they are seen by Nostalgics and Maintainers as playing a slightly deviant role.[8]

Producers will support changes initiated by the executive director that they perceive will enable them to produce more efficiently as individuals. When their own goals coincide with those of the organization, Producers can almost be viewed as part of the Builder group. When Producers' goals are not in concert with those of the nonprofit, however, they give only lip service to organizational goals. Consequently, the executive director can't count on their strong and continued support.

The classic Producer frequently is found in psychological counseling organizations. These counselors usually are committed to their professional identity. They look to that field, not the organization, as the primary source of their professional inspiration. The organization is merely a shell, which they perceive as either facilitating or hindering their individual productivity.

To capitalize upon the Producers' value system, the executive director has to develop a future vision that allows Producers to participate strongly as individual contributors, not as team members. Without such a unifying vision, Producers will continue to be professionally self-centered.

Because the Producer is primarily a strong individual contributor, an executive director can do relatively little to improve the person–organizational relationship. However, the director can try to maximize Producers' efforts in the following ways:

- Channel Producers' vigorous efforts into organizational priorities by linking Producers' special interests to the goals of the nonprofit.
- To the extent possible, provide Producers with the resources needed to be self-managing and productive.
- Whenever possible, remove bureaucratic roadblocks to their productivity.
- Agree annually on goals and let Producers achieve them with a minimum of supervision.

BUILDERS

The difference between Producers and Builders is primarily one of motivation. A Builder, unlike a Producer, is committed to furthering the goals of the organization even at the expense of his or her own personal goals. A top-notch nurse who agrees to become an administrator, even though he or she prefers caring for patients, is an example of a Builder.

In most nonprofits, Builders are a small but energetic group, who fall into one of two categories. Some Builders are *vague visionaries* who get excited about change, while others are *organized progressives* who contribute over the long term to performance improvements.

Vague visionaries enjoy the excitement and exhilaration of something new and different. Unfortunately, their attention shifts rapidly from one detail of a proposed change to another. Consequently, they lack the sustained capacity for completing long-term performance improvements.

The astute executive director uses vague-visionary excitement to fuel the drive for change but doesn't count on vague visionaries for long-range, persistent follow-through on complex improvement efforts. Instead, the director turns to the organized progressives. These individuals are the systematic thinkers in the organization who can quickly develop a sequential picture of when, what, where, and how activities for change will take place. Once they have this picture clearly in mind, organized progressives can provide the executive director with knowledgeable and strong support.

Also of value to an executive director at this juncture are the Producer–Builder hybrids—individuals whose predominant style is that of Producer and whose secondary style is that of Builder. These professionals can bring the values of both groups into play situationally.

Usually the executive director can maximize the values held by the Builder group in the following ways:

- Use the vague-visionary Builders to help sell others when launching new performance programs.
- Explain to organized progressives how their Builder values can contribute to a long-term, systematic improvement plan.
- Give organized progressives strategic follow-up assignments to ensure that new programs move forward.
- Reward Builders who perform well with position and salary upgrades, so that everyone in the organization understands the importance of improving organizational performance.[9]

MANAGING THE FOUR GROUPS

Improvements in organizational performance depend largely on an executive director's ability to use appropriate leadership strategies with the four kinds of professional employees generally found in large, well-established nonprofits. In confronting this challenging problem, an executive director needs to realize that members of the various groups are unlikely to change their value systems, because values are so deeply rooted in individual psychology and life-style. A few employees who are capable of learning from insight may be able to shift from one group to another, for example, from Nostalgic or Maintainer to Producer or Builder. However, such individuals first need to convince themselves—or be convinced—that new work values will produce more total life satisfaction for them.

The executive director's efforts to manage the four groups may lead to some conflict within the organization. A Maintainer may never fully understand, for example, that a Producer's high productivity is the reason that the Producer receives a disproportionately large share of the organization's resources.

It has been our observation that Builders and Producers are in short supply in most organizations, for-profit and nonprofit alike. Executive directors should make every effort to recruit Builders and Producers if they expect their organizations to grow and prosper. And nonprofit boards, in turn, should make every effort to choose a leader of vision—a Builder or at least a hybrid Producer–Builder—to head the organization.

In general, Builders make the most appropriate managers for long-term growth when the environment calls for adaptive change. This is because they easily focus on a continuing stream of new and innovative programs. Yet managerial candidates can rise out of any of the four groups, depending on the individual situation. Often, however, an organization may want to avoid the consequences of choosing a particular kind of person. We know of one nonprofit that appointed a Nostalgic as its senior manager because he was able to claim the support of both Nostalgics and Maintainers on the staff. The outcome was that organizational performance remained static during his long tenure.

Contending creatively with differing groups' performance expectations and performance-linked values will continue to be a challenge for many executive directors through the coming decade.[10] If nonprofits are to continue to serve the nation well, executive directors will need to provide strong support to their Builders and Producers and their value systems. However, if nonprofits are to grow to meet the demands of the future, they must also get as much productivity as possible from their Nostalgic and Maintainer groups.

NOTES

1. Ralph Libby, Barbara Tuchman, and Mark Jensen, "Member Variation, Recognition of Expertise and Group Performances," *Journal of Applied Psychology,* 72 (No. 1, 1987), pp. 81–87.

2. Judith Gordon, *Organizational Behavior: A Diagnostic Approach* (Boston: Allyn & Bacon, 1991), pp. 205–207.

3. Gordon, *Organizational Behavior,* p. 205.

4. Dalamar Fisher, Keith Marron, and William Torbert, "Human Development and Managerial Effectiveness," cited in Gordon, *Organizational Behavior,* pp. 109–115.

5. Gordon, *Organizational Behavior,* pp. 206–207.

6. Gordon, *Organizational Behavior,* p. 405.

7. Peter Drucker, *Managing the Nonprofit Organization* (New York: Harper Collins, 1990), p. 147.

8. Gordon, *Organizational Behavior,* p. 207.

9. Gordon, *Organizational Behavior,* p. 742.

10. Drucker, *Managing the Nonprofit Organization,* pp. 107–142.

6

TERMINATING THE INEFFECTIVE EXECUTIVE DIRECTOR

Unable to sleep, Jim Stoneham, a board member of XYZ Social Agency, reluctantly goes to his kitchen for a 4 A.M. cup of coffee. He hopes the coffee will clear his muddled thoughts. It's been a day and a half since that unsettling telephone call from Sarah Michaels, board chairperson of the agency, but snatches of the conversation still haunt him.

"Harry's a great guy, even a dedicated executive director, but he's not able to do the job for us. Despite the strong support we've given him, he's not performing well. There's no hope, Jim. I think it's time we told him so. We're responsible if this organization falls apart. The way things are going, we are certainly headed in that direction."

Jim knew he hadn't given Sarah an answer. The conversation was one-sided because he didn't know what to say, and he wanted more time to mull over the problem.

He was uncomfortable being involved in terminating the top executive of the nonprofit agency. As a professor at the local university, he had never been involved in such management activities. He agreed with Sarah, but he genuinely liked Harry as a person and respected him as a humanitarian.

Jim Stoneham should be familiar to a great many of us. His concerns and struggle to decide how to proceed with sensitivity and fairness are not unique. With about one million nonprofit organizations in the United States, his dilemma is probably duplicated hundreds, maybe even thousands of times each year.

Just how does a nonprofit board, consisting of individuals from diverse walks of life and backgrounds, act effectively and humanely when it must terminate the employment of its top operating manager?

Such termination decisions and actions are the most difficult duties that a nonprofit board must handle. The termination can't be delegated, and it must be fair and equitable. And, it is important to note, the employment and dismissal of the executive director are the only personnel *operating actions* that nonprofit boards properly should take. In all other matters, the board should be concerned with policy, not personnel, issues.[1]

COMMON PERFORMANCE PROBLEMS

Board members can't effectively handle termination of a top manager until they learn to analyze the key elements and factors, both external and internal, that make for ineffective performance at the executive level.

INABILITY TO CHANGE

Some executive directors do a fine job for years but then settle into the job and no longer demonstrate vigor or vision. They don't fully recognize significant differences in their external environment, such as changes in funding resources, shifts in community interest, reduced support for the organization's services or products, or increased competition from either the nonprofit or the for-profit sector.

Although the organization may appear to operate effectively, it is already in a slow decline. What is not perceived by

the stable but ineffective executive director is that serious difficulties are just around the corner. This type of problem with top
management has accelerated in the past decade and is particularly apparent in certain nonprofit arenas. For example, in the
day-care and home-nursing-services fields, until recently the
domain of nonprofits, executive directors could be courting disaster if they fail to develop new ways to meet the challenges
posed by highly competitive for-profit groups.

LACK OF REQUISITE LEADERSHIP SKILLS

The road to a top management job in nonprofits is traditionally by way of the slow process of acculturation. Typically, the
direct-service employee, such as a social work counselor, initially
is given some supervisory or management responsibilities while
continuing with direct-service obligations. Too often this hybrid
position means the individual retains his or her direct-service
identity, while management activities are secondary concerns.

Though the person's supervisory or management responsibilities increase, he or she continues to identify primarily with the
direct-service role. He or she never develops into an effective
manager, even though given the title of executive director. Consequently, the organization's management productivity is limited
by the executive's inadequate leadership skills. As the performance gap widens, termination often becomes the only solution.

INEFFECTIVE CONFLICT MANAGEMENT

Some conflict is inevitable and healthy in any organization. Ineffective executive directors, however, often lack the
skills to mobilize joint problem-solving efforts in response to
organizational conflicts.[2] As a result, manipulative trade-offs or
outright "win–lose" conflicts ensue. Such conflicts can arise

from diverse sources, including staff, the board, and even the community.

Staff conflict may develop when the executive director is insensitive to or unaware of staff concerns. Or a top executive may fail to communicate well with the changing population one finds on nonprofit boards. As a result, a board-versus-executive director power struggle can develop on one or more issues and result in a termination action. In a few rare instances, executive directors come in conflict with funding personnel or community and industry leaders. Such conflict is obviously not healthy. When it begins to harm the productivity of the nonprofit, a termination action by the board is in order.

HEALTH CONCERNS

Deteriorating health as the basis for contemplating termination of an executive director is perhaps the most difficult situation board members face. It is not uncommon for a top manager to want to stay on the job, even when he or she is dealing with serious health problems that significantly affect performance. Although fairness and compassion are important issues in such cases, a painful human process must be endured by the board that decides termination is necessary.

REVERED BUT INCOMPETENT

Some ineffective managers retain their position for a time simply because they have pleasant personalities and friendly relationships. At some point, however, the needs of the organization grow beyond warm, friendly leadership. Often, problems surface when a crisis occurs: funding is severely reduced or managerial requirements of the organization change in a way that the person is unable or unwilling to handle.

71

PRE-TERMINATION ACTIVITIES

Before a board decides to terminate its executive director for inadequate performance, it should take all of the standard preliminary steps. These basic steps include:

- Formal evaluation of the executive's accomplishments against goals
- Written notification of professional or personal deficiencies
- Reasonable board support to assist in removing deficiencies over time

Even the most casual observer of the nonprofit scene will note that these basic steps are frequently either ignored or poorly executed by boards seeking to terminate an executive. This is because of the variety of backgrounds one finds in nonprofit board leadership and because of the frequent changes in leadership on some boards. Some trade associations appoint new volunteer presidents every year.

Some stories of executive director termination are painful. One termination with which we are familiar took place barely six months after the incumbent received an excellent performance review. In other cases, executive directors have had a poor performance review shortly after some significant professional achievement.

Pre-termination steps should be handled in a systematic and administratively sound manner. Executive directors who are dismissed have every right to expect fair and professional treatment throughout the termination process. When dismissal is inevitable, the following process will help a board complete the successful termination of an ineffective executive director and help ease the inevitable pain involved in this kind of personnel action.

SEVEN STEPS TO A SUCCESSFUL TERMINATION

Assuming an executive director is being terminated because he or she is ineffective, and not due to illegal, immoral, or dishonest activities, the following seven steps can help to create a positive organizational climate, even in the midst of a difficult personnel action. The board, moving through the steps in order, must:

- Confront the problem
- Develop board consensus
- Develop community or industry support
- Plan the termination
- Arrange for greater board involvement
- Initiate personal discussions
- Develop a public and internal posture concerning the termination

CONFRONT THE PROBLEM

Several board leaders must closely examine the situation and determine whether the board has done everything within reason to remedy leadership and/or management problems. These individuals must be satisfied that the board has not interfered with management or been part of the problem.[3]

Most important, they must be willing to encourage others on the board to deal with the situation. This is not always easy. Even the most sophisticated board members with extensive management experience may be reluctant to become involved in the conflict. Because their responsibility to the nonprofit board does not involve any financial or personal risk, they may avoid actions that can lead to strife. This may be true even though they acknowledge that terminating the executive director is the only way to achieve reasonable organizational productivity.

DEVELOP BOARD CONSENSUS

This step requires that a majority of the board agree that employment termination is the best solution. Expect that some board members will want to give the executive "one more chance." These individuals sincerely believe that not everything possible has been done to support the executive director. In addition, expect some board members to be reluctant to take strong direct action that will cause the executive short-term career distress.

However, boards that use a compassionate approach to director termination can develop a positive outcome. The staff, the community, and possibly the terminated executive director can feel that the situation has been handled in a fair and equitable manner. The individual's dignity and self-worth are preserved. If all members of the board feel the dismissal process is being handled equitably, fewer intergroup board hostilities will develop.

When a strong—which means total—consensus can't be reached about terminating the executive, the possibility exists that the board will become divided. Whether the termination process goes forward or is halted, such polarization allows for two or more hostile board subgroups to emerge. When this type of board conflict occurs, angry resignations may occur. The subsequent healing process may take several years to be completed. In some instances, a divided board is inevitable. However, every effort should be made to avoid negative feelings through the use of joint problem-solving efforts regarding the termination action.

DEVELOP COMMUNITY OR INDUSTRY SUPPORT

More than an organization's employees are affected when a top manager is dismissed. In the case of human service organizations, members of the wider community will also be concerned about the impending change. In a professional group or trade association, the membership will be affected. Consequently, selected leaders in the wider community—be it town, industry, or profession—must be advised of the impending move. For example, if the organization is supported by the local United Way, the top person in the United Way needs advance notice of the situation. In a trade association, leaders of some of the major firms affected need to be apprised of the coming change.

If community or industry support is not obtained, a public relations problem may develop that can take considerable time and effort to remedy. Developing such support is particularly important when the person being terminated is well liked. Reinstatement of the executive director can become the cause of special-interest groups. Adverse public reaction to an executive's firing can affect the operations of the organization and the work of the new executive director for a long time.

PLAN THE TERMINATION

The board or the board's executive committee needs to agree on the broad parameters of the dismissal before the executive director is informed of the board's decision. The plan should include severance pay or other financial considerations, the length of time insurance benefits will be continued, the effective date of any "resignation," outplacement or job-hunting support, office support, and other issues pertinent to a high-level termination.

75

The scope of the plan will obviously depend on the executive director's length of service and his or her contributions to the organization. However, the level of personal guilt on the board will also be a factor. Particularly if the board has done a poor job of pre-termination evaluation, the guilt level of some board members will tend to be high. Very often, overly generous severance packages are offered to compensate for such guilt feelings.

A separate question the board must answer is "How long should the executive director who has been dismissed continue to manage the organization?" Some boards will choose to have the incumbent leave the organization the day he or she is informed of the board's decision. Other boards will opt to have the individual continue to work until a mutually agreed date, up to and including the actual "resignation" date.

ARRANGE FOR GREATER BOARD INVOLVEMENT

Whatever approach is used, the board must be ready immediately to assume more direct responsibility for the operations of the organization. This, it is hoped, should be only for a short period. The most promising scenario calls instead for a staff subordinate to assume the position on an acting basis with strong guidance from the board or a board committee. Another alternative is to engage, in the interim before a new executive is hired, an outside person with the necessary experience, such as a recent retiree. The interim executive director needs to work under the guidance of a special board committee, with meetings taking place as often as every week or 10 days.

In any top-level termination, the need for direct board involvement in operations escalates considerably. However, each nonprofit board must recognize that when it appoints a successor, its focus turns once again from operations to policy issues.[4]

INITIATE PERSONAL DISCUSSIONS

The board president should inform the executive director of the board's decision to dismiss him or her. At that time, the president should present the conditions of the termination and answer questions. All conditions should be presented in detail and in writing. The president should be empowered to make minor modifications to the conditions and should also be able to receive quick feedback from the board on concerns of a significant nature. If desirable, the assistance of an outplacement organization could be offered immediately following the termination meeting. The interpersonal approach known as supporting–confronting is most likely to produce a win–win outcome. When this approach is taken, the executive is confronted with the performance gap that led to his or her dismissal, but the board president is careful not to attack the executive as an individual.[5]

DEVELOP A PUBLIC AND INTERNAL POSTURE

After the personal discussions are complete, the board president should have a prepared announcement ready to inform the community or industry of the organization's change in leadership. The final plan should be developed in conjunction with the terminated executive director to enhance his or her probability of finding another position. Consequently, such issues as allowing for a sabbatical, vacation, or consulting relationship need to be discussed. Appropriate board action will help create a positive public image concerning the termination.

THE SUCCESSFUL TERMINATION

Three sets of skills help nonprofit boards deal effectively with the issue of terminating an executive director's employment. The first involves the use of sound human-resources-management, performance-appraisal, and development systems. Together they provide an objective basis for evaluation of the director's performance and termination when performance is inadequate.

The second set of skills involves the seven-step process described in this chapter, along with the application of a fair and compassionate approach to create a positive climate for termination.

The final set of skills is interpersonal. Conflict-resolution methods should be employed to avoid hostile actions and intergroup conflict among various constituencies.

To achieve the results desired, the nonprofit board must be certain that all pre-termination evaluations have been completed and that the recommended seven-step process is chosen as the model for board action. If all of these steps are taken, the board is likely to create a situation that will allow for a smooth transition to a new management team.

NOTES

1. Eugene H. Fram with Vicki Brown, *Policy vs. Paper Clips: Selling the Corporate Model to Your Nonprofit Board* (Milwaukee, WI: Family Service America, 1988); Richard P. Chait and Barbara E. Taylor, "Charting the Territory of Nonprofit Boards," *Harvard Business Review* 89 (January–February, 1989), pp. 44–54.

2. Daniel Druckerman, "New Directions for a Social Psychology of Conflict," in Dennis Sandole and Richard Beckhard, eds., *Conflict Manage-*

ment and Problem Solving (New York: New York University Press, 1987).

3. Fram, *Policy vs. Paper Clips.*

4. Fram, *Policy vs. Paper Clips*; Chait and Taylor, "Charting the Territory."

5. David Whetton and Kim Cameron, *Developing Managerial Skills* (New York: Harper Collins, 1991).

7

BUILDING THE SLIM AND SMART NONPROFIT ORGANIZATION

A nonprofit organization that is not changing to meet the demands of the 1990s is an organization that is ignoring reality, wasting precious time, and possibly courting disaster.

The business world has numerous examples of companies that waited too long to change and therefore were forced to opt for crisis management over careful planning and implementation. Some of these firms survived, some didn't, and some don't yet know what the outcome will be. Nonprofits should learn from the experiences of others and pay attention to the lessons of the for-profit sector in order to reduce the possibility of being hurt in similar crisis situations.

In particular, nonprofits must revise and restructure operations in response to the new environmental realities that they face. As noted earlier, some of the important environmental forces causing nonprofits to adjust include:

- The overlap of service offerings between private nonprofit groups and for-profit organizations (and sometimes even governmental agencies)
- The increase in competition among all nonprofit organizations for a share of a shrinking funding base
- The need to use marketing strategies to "sell" organizational products and services to both clients and other stakeholders, including donors, foundations, and volunteers

■ The change in demographic patterns

These and other external environmental changes have presented nonprofits with both exciting opportunities and serious concerns. They have caused the expansion of some nonprofits and the downsizing of others. For example, the growth in the need for nursing homes has enabled some nursing-home nonprofits to expand to multicorporation units offering different levels of care. Similarly, the American Association of Retired Persons (AARP) has capitalized on the needs of the growing number of older Americans to become the second largest nonprofit in the nation. Currently, AARP has more than 30 million members and is growing at a rate of some two million to three million members a year.

Other nonprofits have responded to environmental challenges by establishing profit-making subsidiaries to generate new revenues in order to fill the financial gap between expenses and income. An enterprising hospital in Miami, Florida, markets its own brand of chicken soup. Other examples include the University of Florida, which has earned $17 million in royalties since 1972 from the sale of Gatorade; the Association for the Blind, which turned some sheltered workshops into profitable enterprises; and various nonprofits that have opened retail stores.

Unfortunately for some nonprofits, the new realities have meant their organizations must downsize through restructuring. In downsizing, they have followed a route traveled by many profit-making firms in the recent past. This route involves the well-known processes of cutting costs, increasing work loads, and selling assets.

Downsizing has occurred as the result of a "lean and mean" business philosophy and strategy, a rough, hatchet-like approach based on crisis management.[1] Although such an approach has been helpful to some companies in the short term, it has had negative long-term consequences for many. The Chrysler Corporation and Sears, Roebuck & Co. are notable examples of for-profits with lean and mean management strategies that appeared successful initially but seem less attractive over time as competition has escalated. Both firms face substantial challenges and observers wait, with considerable interest, to observe the longer-term strategic outcomes.

THE SLIM AND SMART ALTERNATIVE

An alternative to lean and mean is the "slim and smart" approach.[2] This approach does not involve specific steps but instead calls for management to develop an overall transitional framework and climate for the organization. It does, however, require planning with sufficient lead time.

Using this alternative, the organization takes a longer view. Its leaders must enlist motivated and committed staff to help reduce some of the negative effects of downsizing. In implementing such a program, management develops a framework for a well-thought-out downsizing plan. Such a slim and smart plan provides a series of actions that a nonprofit can take to cope with anticipated personnel and financial problems.

In academia, for example, a few visionary universities began years ago to plan for the anticipated reduction in college-age students that would affect their enrollment patterns in the 1990s. They took significant steps to ensure that curricula were up to date and attractive and they eliminated marginal programs. Steps were also taken to retain their top faculty members, and careful long-range plans were laid to improve

84

campus physical facilities. In addition, faculty and staff were involved in preparing for a different kind of campus learning environment and new kinds of challenges. Now, the number of college-age students is extremely low, as anticipated, and these schools will be able to evaluate how successful their strategic-planning frameworks have been. They can also see the colleges that failed to plan facing very serious enrollment crises in the current decade.

Underlying the slim and smart approach is the "what's fair?" business ethic. This ethic promotes managerial actions that attempt to provide equitable treatment for all persons affected by downsizing. Hewlett-Packard, for example, has not been immune to economic downturns in recent years, but has approached the problem by asking everyone in the corporation to take a moderate pay cut or by asking all employees to postpone raises. As a consequence, the employees have perceived the changes as being necessary and relevant. They've also seen that no special employee group has benefited from the sacrifices of others.

Other businesses have employed the "what's fair?" ethic in different ways. Examples include shifting employees who might otherwise be laid off to open positions, rather than hiring new personnel, and working to retain productive employees.

The thrust of all activities in a slim and smart strategy is to get a high level of managerial and staff performance and to have every individual's efforts directed toward providing quality client services. To improve performance, slim and smart organizations use high-performance management techniques, such as the highly regarded Total Quality Management (TQM) approach mentioned in chapter 1.

The numerous aspects of TQM that slim and smart organizations employ include:

- **Empowerment,** which involves a reduction in hierarchical authority and the development of individual and team creativity
- **Continuous quality improvement,** which calls for personnel continually to move from present performance to a higher level of performance
- **Zero defects,** yet another way to satisfy customers and meet requirements
- **Teamwork,** using self-managing work groups or interdepartmental teams to solve problems and motivate individuals[3]

If personnel in a nonprofit that successfully adopts a Total Quality program are capable of handling these types of performance responsibilities, they can take creative actions to improve performance. However, in some nonprofits the empowerment process may be hampered by long-standing work-group values, such as those of the Maintainers described in chapter 5.

BASIC STEPS IN THE STRATEGY

To move in the slim and smart direction, board members and top management must first examine the organization's external environment, then identify available resources and marketing opportunities.

Examining the changing nature of the organization's external environment requires a thorough self-study. The examination should review the current performance status of the organization as well as how the organization is viewed by colleagues, clients, and others. It should also consider the probable impact of emerging societal and technological forces during the coming years.

Like any individual undertaking self-analysis, it is important for the organization to be realistic about itself. In some cases, an outside consultant may be needed to help the board and management determine whether the organization's performance is seen by colleagues and/or clients as outstanding, average, or below average. Some top nonprofit managers may find this type of review wrenching. They may be uncomfortable accepting valid, but uncomplimentary, feedback from colleagues, clients, and stakeholders. Yet open analysis and discussion of the current state of affairs are essential.

It is strategically important to estimate what changes in society or in technological capability will affect the organization most strongly. An organization that exists to serve a cause —for instance, the polio epidemic was the catalyst for the March of Dimes—must determine what its future will be if its primary cause is either diminished or eliminated.

Such issues affect many nonprofits in both the social service and trade association categories. For example, the development of a polio vaccine caused the March of Dimes to change its primary focus from polio to birth defects. Similarly, technology has changed in the photofinishing industry, and nonprofit trade groups that serve the industry have changed their services to fit the needs of one-hour photofinishers instead of medium-sized production organizations.

When a nonprofit examines its role, it should be asking the hard questions that will shape its future. One might ask, for example, what will be the impact in 10 years on the current mission of the Red Cross if scientists are successful in developing artificial blood?

The organization taking steps to become slim and smart must also realistically assess what resources are available to it.

Resources fall into financial, staff, management, and equipment categories.

For a nonprofit, the issue of current and future funding is almost always the most critical. Organizations that are highly dependent on government funding must consider ways to live within a restricted funding environment or find creative ways to develop new revenue sources.

When employee cutbacks must be made as part of downsizing, the slim and smart organization will look for ways to retain its high-performing personnel. Retention of such personnel can be a real challenge, because they are usually the employees with the most professional mobility. To keep them, management will have to be creative in developing both monetary and nonmonetary incentives. Working with the board, the executive director will need to determine what will motivate the best people in the organization, keep them on the job, and continue to encourage them to perform at a high level.

The final objective of the slim and smart nonprofit—looking for marketing opportunities—requires the organization to find new ways to serve current clients or seek new client groups that can be served within the present resource structure. This objective requires, as do the two earlier steps, the executive director to create a supportive organizational climate in which employees can pursue new and different markets. For example, some for-profit day-care centers are experimenting with offering dry cleaning drop-off services and video rentals.

GETTING YOUR ORGANIZATION READY

Getting an organization ready for a period of downsizing by means of the slim and smart approach requires an organizational vision based on client requirements and stakeholder expectations. Also critical are willing employees who understand the leadership's vision and can meet the challenges it poses. Not only do employees need to see the vision as a viable one, but they must also be able to form collaborative teams and become involved in the downsizing process. It is unrealistic to assume that every employee will be fully committed to the vision, but a substantial portion must be if downsizing efforts are to be successful.

The board and senior management personnel need to assess carefully the organization's readiness for change. They must determine whether all members of the organization acknowledge that restructuring is required and are aware of the challenges involved. If the organization is not ready to accept necessary changes, the board and top management must jointly develop an educational program to create awareness of the need for change. Although this may take time, it is not wise to attempt to transform the organization when such awareness is not present.

In addition to getting the organization ready for change, board and top management must identify high-performance goals that can be subscribed to by a significant number of employees. These goals can range from increasing productivity and lowering costs to establishing experimental programs and offering new client services. In some instances, the goals might even involve radical change in the mission of the nonprofit.

Inevitably, conflicts will arise in the process of becoming a slim and smart, high-performance nonprofit. When internal conflict occurs, open negotiation can help create "win–win" outcomes. The most difficult situations involve termination of employees. However, management's adoption of the "what's fair?" ethic early in the process helps to reduce, though not eliminate, this type of conflict. For example, management might consider offering some employees a reduced work week rather than termination, with the provision that their situation will be reviewed within a specified period. Management might also consider special options for long-term employees who are nearing retirement age.

Management should be prepared, however, for some intergroup conflicts to regress to the "win–lose" level. In such cases, the executive director should attempt to use conflict-resolution techniques to minimize the impact of the struggle.

Finally, top management must be certain that its interdepartmental teams are broad based and empowered to confront problems, for it is these teams that will make TQM or other client-centered approaches work. The key is to make certain that team activities center on quality issues and performance improvement rather than on interpersonal politics. Eventually the existence of such teams should improve performance by reducing the amount of unnecessary bureaucracy in the nonprofit, which, in turn, should result in better service for clients. Planning and operations will be driven by client and stakeholder requirements, not bureaucratic needs.

All of the steps outlined here assume that the organization has the necessary lead time to make transitional changes. If this is not the case, the only alternative is crisis management, which is typically accompanied by serious organizational and interpersonal turmoil.

THE ROLE OF THE EXECUTIVE DIRECTOR

The executive director plays a key role in meeting a downsizing challenge and developing a slim and smart organization. Specifically, the executive director must:

■ **Assist the board in developing the vision statement.** The executive director is, after all, the most knowledgeable person in the organization about trends in the areas served by the nonprofit. Like a good teacher, he or she should help guide the discussions of the board in developing the vision statement.

■ **Develop a small but representative subgroup of employees to win organizational support for the new vision.** The executive director, not the board, must be the focus of transformation in a slim and smart nonprofit. Consequently, he or she needs to form a committee or task force to support the effort. Typically, the task force is a working group of 8 to 10 members, drawn from a cross-section of employees who are committed to the organization. Task force members should be thoughtful individuals and good communicators. The members of the group should become the key communicators and staff liaisons for the project as it evolves.

■ **Be persistent.** All members of the organization will not accept the need for high performance or organizational downsizing. Consequently, a high level of persistence in managing the change process will be needed. In some instances, job termination will be the only answer to those who simply refuse to be a part of the new reality.

■ **Secure the proper balance between employee empowerment and participation and the need for managerial authority.** Although the slim and smart approach to downsizing encourages greater employee participation than is common in many nonprofit organizations, this involvement must be balanced with a reasonable amount of hierarchical control. After the interdepartmental groups come to their final conclusions about changes and improvements, executive decisions will ultimately be made by top managers and the board. Employees must understand how the consultative process works and be prepared to accept management decisions. It is up to the executive director to prepare staff personnel for these prospects and to educate them about the difference between a consultative management approach and participative management. Consultative management encourages broad joint problem solving, but the executive director and board have the final decision power. In full participative management, higher managers are prepared to accept all changes recommended by task teams, regardless of merit.

■ **Keep the focus on clients and stakeholders.** Every organization faces the danger of becoming overly involved with group processes. Because the slim and smart approach is participant driven, groups can easily confuse the process with results. It is the executive director's job to make sure that client or stakeholder requirements are not only the focus of the process, but also the reason for its end products.

■ **Develop rigorous benchmark standards.** The approach to high performance requires that an organization establish benchmarks by which it can judge its growth. External benchmarks are often based upon the achievements of other organizations within the field. For example, a nonprofit day-care center might measure its employee performance standards against those of a profit-making day-care center. To obtain high-performance results, the executive must know what performance levels are being achieved by other organizations and how these might be used as appropriate benchmarks for his or her group.

■ **Monitor progress.** Because the executive director is central to restructuring based on the slim and smart approach, he or she will need to make certain that realistic progress is being made. Deadlines and timetables need to be established so that concrete results can be achieved. Without proper monitoring, the nonprofit's "process addicts" can drive discussions about change and improvements in circles for long periods of time. This results in little substantive output.

■ **Build a continuous-improvement culture.** Develop an organizational climate in which employees value and strive for continuous improvement in operating methods and customer service.[4]

In the final analysis, how well a slim and smart approach to downsizing works depends on two things: whether adequate lead time is available and how effectively the executive director manages the options for improvement and change. Because the approach can utilize different types of employee involvement, the overall management expertise of the executive director is a key factor in the successful outcome of the venture.

There are no easy paths to high performance. Our society now—and in the next century—needs high-performance nonprofit organizations. Intelligent and perceptive managers are the key to leading employees in the process of building such groups.

NOTES

1. "America's Leanest and Meanest," *Business Week,* October 5, 1987, p. 78.

2. Robert Pearse and Herbert Jarvis, "Corporate Restructuring in a Casino Society," *New Management,* 3 (Summer 1988), pp. 55–60.

3. Richard J. Schoenberger, *Building a Chain of Customers—Linking Business Functions to Create the World Class Company* (New York: Free Press, 1990).

4. David T. Kearns, "Welcoming Remarks," *Proceedings from the Xerox Quality Forum II* (Stamford, CT: Xerox Corporation, July 31–August 2, 1990).

A

SAMPLE EXECUTIVE DIRECTOR POSITION DESCRIPTION

POSITION

The executive director is responsible to the board of directors. He or she serves as the principal professional liaison to the board and its chief officer. In cooperation with the chief officer of the board, the executive director represents the organization in contacts with community, business, and governmental leaders. The executive director will be expected to apply appropriate knowledge, skills, and behaviors in the following performance areas:

HUMAN RESOURCE ACTIVITIES

- In conjunction with the board, assures continuity of top-level volunteer direction for the organization through a program of cultivation, recruitment, and motivation of board members.
- Assists volunteer leadership to identify problems that relate to client concerns.
- Manages all personnel activities, including recruitment, selection, placement, training, development, performance evaluation, and promotion of staff.
- Plans his or her own professional development.

STRATEGIC PLANNING AND IMPLEMENTATION

- Cultivates and develops cooperative relationships necessary to fund and implement effective services.
- Enhances public understanding and support of organizational activities through a coordinated communications program.

- Develops a positive, productive organizational culture and climate. This includes defining the organization's vision, mission, and the role of employee participation.
- Develops short- and long-range plans for organizational growth and continuity.
- Develops strategic marketing plans for enhancement of the organization's services and image.
- With the board, monitors the organization's market position and its structure to meet organizational goals.

FINANCIAL MANAGEMENT

- Manages financial resources, including operating budget and collection, disbursement, and accounting for all funds, property, and official records.
- Works with board and supervises staff on fund-raising and other resource-development activities.
- Maintains tight financial controls on a cost–benefit basis in accordance with accepted accounting procedures.
- Manages cash flow in a conservative manner.

OPERATIONS MANAGEMENT

- Establishes organizational plans, policies, and procedures as necessary for effective operation of the organization.
- Manages and directs the activities of staff engaged in the following activities: (list organization's programs).
- Develops effective and efficient support systems for the organization, including computer services, training, personnel, purchasing, and management information.
- Establishes and maintains effective and efficient delivery systems.
- Makes effective use of supplies, equipment, and space.

Note: The executive director's position description should reflect the nonprofit's current leadership requirements. A position description and related job qualifications should be related realistically to the immediate and long-range goals of the organization. The personal qualities, education, and specific experience needed for the executive director position are particular to each organization and should be described in additional sections.

B

CHECKLIST FOR SCREENING CANDIDATES

The checklist on the following pages is for search committee members to utilize in a first review of resumes submitted in application for the executive director position. It should help committee members choose applications that meet the committee's criteria for qualifications.

This list allows individual reviewers to note whether an applicant has relevant education or experience in a number of areas. It also allows for additional strengths to be mentioned by reviewers.

The list is generic. It should be modified by individual search committees to reflect the criteria and qualifications that they have set for their specific executive director position.

The list is intended to capsulize the strengths of each candidate. Each committee member should use the list to review strengths noted in individual resumes and attach the completed list to the resume as a summary. The full committee should then eliminate from consideration those resumes in which relatively few strengths are noted.

Candidate's Name: _____

Reviewer's Name: _____

Education

☐ Advanced degree in appropriate area
☐ Continued education in areas related to job description (administration, planning, fund raising, development, community relations, etc.)

Relevance of Organizational Experience

☐ Experience in nonprofit organization
☐ Experience in this type of organization
☐ Experience in an organization providing one or more of the other programs offered by our organization

Supervisory Experience

☐ Experience in supervising support and professional staff
☐ Experience in goal setting for and evaluation of staff
☐ Experience in staff-development programs

Board Experience

☐ Experience staffing a board or advisory committee
☐ Participation on special board–staff committees
☐ Experience in preparing and presenting materials to a board

Program Administration

☐ Experience in planning programs
☐ Experience in organizing/establishing programs
☐ Experience in monitoring/evaluating programs
☐ Experience in financial administration

Human Resources Administration

- ☐ Experience in personnel administration, including the hiring, training, and development of employees
- ☐ Experience in salary administration
- ☐ Experience in fringe-benefit administration

Development

- ☐ Experience in preparing proposals for funding and refunding
- ☐ Experience in presenting applications to and negotiation with foundations and/or other funding sources
- ☐ Experience in planning, organizing, and executing fund-raising events with boards and staff.

Community/Public Relations

- ☐ Experience in contact with community, trade association, and government leaders and groups
- ☐ Experience in representing the organization in contacts with community and/or business groups
- ☐ Experience in publicizing organization services
- ☐ Experience in serving on other boards

Planning

- ☐ Experience in exploring new program areas
- ☐ Experience in assessing and prioritizing needs within organization
- ☐ Experience in assessing needs within community, industry, or profession

Executive

- ☐ Previous experience as an executive director (note size of staff and budget; types of programs offered)

Miscellaneous

- ☐ At least two years' tenure with most previous employers
- ☐ Promotions by previous employers
- ☐ Job pattern of increasing responsibilities
- ☐ Job pattern of varied tasks in both direct service and management
- ☐ Membership in professional organizations
- ☐ Membership in community, religious, or fraternal organizations

Other Strengths of Candidate

_____

_____

_____

_____

_____

_____

_____

_____

_____

_____

_____

_____

_____

_____

_____

_____

_____

C

INFORMATION PACKAGE FOR INTERVIEWEES

The search committee should assemble a package of information about the organization and the community in which it is located. All finalists should receive this material to prepare them for personal interviews. The following suggests the kind of material that should be included in such a package.

- Roster of search committee, including relevant backgrounds and/or professional affiliations of members
- Position description
- Annual report
- Annual audit report and management letter
- Budget summary
- Roster of board of directors, including title and professional affiliation of each member
- Bylaws
- Organizational chart, including volunteers and staff
- Personnel policies
- Special reports, i.e., long-range planning report, management evaluation report
- Chamber of Commerce package or other descriptive material on community

D

INTERVIEW ASSESSMENT GUIDE

The simple, nonnumerical rating sheet below may be used during or after each candidate's personal interview to record the interviewer's reaction to the candidate's performance *vis-à-vis* a predetermined set of criteria and qualifications. The essential and desirable qualifications and criteria developed by the search committee can be recorded under the appropriate headings. This guide should be used in conjunction with Appendix E.

Criteria	Candidate's Name	Candidate's Name	Candidate's Name
Essential knowledge, skills, behaviors			
1.			
2.			
3.			
4.			
5.			
Desirable but not essential knowledge, skills, behaviors			
1.			
2.			
3.			
4.			
5.			

Scoring symbols: + = exceeds expectations; 0 = meets expectations; – = does not meet expectations; ? = needs more follow-up information.

E

SAMPLE INTERVIEW QUESTIONS

The following is a list of criteria and sample questions to be used by search committee members during the personal interview with each candidate. These questions can be used "as is" or adapted to the specific criteria and qualifications for an organization's executive director position. All interview questions must conform to equal opportunity and affirmative action guidelines. Committee members in doubt about these guidelines should consult an experienced human resources professional.

Leadership Skills

Exhibits the ability to motivate, inspire loyalty, demonstrate creative approaches to problems and issues, be comfortable with both superiors and subordinates. Creates a positive interpersonal climate for the organization.

Sample Interview Questions:

- What is your approach to identifying and recruiting volunteers?
- How would you generate and maintain a high level of board motivation and commitment?
- How would you generate and maintain a high level of staff motivation and commitment?
- What has been the most difficult problem or issue you have faced in your current position? How have you dealt with it?

Management Skills

Demonstrates the ability to plan, organize, direct, and control. Successful experience supervising and developing staff. Willingness to delegate responsibility and authority. Has working knowledge of financial and personnel administration, strategic and tactical planning techniques.

Sample Interview Questions:

- Please give us a brief characterization of your management style.
- Do you have a work plan in your current position? How did you go about developing it?
- What changes have you made or helped effect in your present organization?
- What do you feel is the ideal staff and/or volunteer structure for this type of organization?
- Have you had experience in developing and implementing a budget? Tell us about it.
- Have you had experience in salary and benefit administration? Tell us about it.
- How would you design a system for staff evaluation?

Familiarity with the Nonprofit Sector and Volunteer/Staff Roles

Has been a staff member in a nonprofit organization. Understands the need for nonprofit services. Understands the difference between staff and volunteer roles and responsibilities.

Sample Interview Questions:

- What is your view of the appropriate role of staff and volunteers? How do they relate?
- How, in your view, should nonprofit and governmental services interrelate?
- What do you feel are the most important issues facing the nonprofit sector?

Fund Raising/Public Relations

Has worked with board and staff in successfully planning, organizing, and executing a fund-raising event. Has skills in proposal writing. Has knowledge and skills pertaining to marketing an organization's programs. Has knowledge and skills applicable to the development of new sources of funding.

Sample Interview Questions:

- Tell us about your fund-raising experience. How would that experience apply here?
- How would you go about developing the rationale for support of this type of organization?
- Have you developed proposals for funding or refunding?
- Have you had experience in presenting proposals to foundations, the United Way, or other funding sources?

Commitment to the Field

Comes from a service organization or has made a conscious, well-thought-out decision to change careers.

Sample Interview Questions:

- How would our executive director position fit into your career plan?
- Career-wise, where do you see yourself in five years? In ten years?

Oral Communication Skills

Experience in public speaking. Appears to be articulate, persuasive. Thinks and responds quickly and concisely. Listens with comprehension and empathy.

Sample Interview Questions:

- How much public speaking is required in your current

position?

■ Have you presented information on your organization to outside groups?

Knowledge of Issues Facing Nonprofit Organizations

Can articulate key issues and has formed opinions about them and about approaches to dealing with them. Examples: federal funding cutbacks, unionization of staff, competition with for-profit organizations.

Sample Interview Questions:

■ What do you feel are key issues facing our type of organization?

■ What approaches would you take to dealing with these issues?

Staffing Boards and Committees

Knows the structure and function of the board of directors, executive committee, and other committees of a typical nonprofit board. Has experience in planning, organizing, and providing staff support to committees dealing with significant issues. Understands the dynamics of committees and the leadership and support roles of staff.

Sample Interview Questions:

■ Do you staff any board committees in your current position?

■ How would you generally prepare volunteer board members for their committee assignments?

■ Sometimes committees conflict or reach an impasse. Have you experienced these situations? How would you resolve them?

■ When do you feel a problem or issue should be handled by a committee rather than by an individual?

- (Present an issue or problem.) How would you go about dealing with this problem or issue through the committee process?
- Do you serve on any boards? Tell us about your experience.

Utilization of Volunteers

Successfully matches volunteer board members with tasks that are appropriate to their interests, skills, and position in the community. Understands creative ways to involve volunteers.

Sample Interview Questions:

- How does your organization identify and select volunteers for the board, committees, and task forces? What has been your role in this identification and selection?
- How would you harness and maintain the interest of top community leadership?
- How would you recognize and reward volunteer participation in an organization?

Continuing Education and Training

Exhibits growth and development through job-related education and training courses.

Sample Interview Questions:

- In what way do you continue to develop your knowledge and skills?
- What design for executive evaluation do you prefer?
- Do you have a career-development plan?

Staff-Development Experience

Successful experience in supervising, evaluating, and developing staff. Experience with professional education programs.

Sample Interview Questions:

- What design for staff evaluation do you prefer?
- Tell us about your experience with staff development.
- What design for professional supervision do you prefer?

Planning

Has worked with board, staff, and community or industry representatives in program or long-range planning. Has reviewed and monitored programs. Has developed new programs. Has experience with management information systems.

Sample Interview Questions:

- How would you go about assessing our community, industry, or profession's needs and deciding what role our organization should have in meeting them?
- Having received a description of our organization's current programs, describe any shortcomings you see and/or changes you might propose in them.
- How would you plan and develop a program for this organization? (List program area into which the organization might expand.)
- Tell us about your experience with management information systems.
- In your present position, from where do you receive planning information? How do you use it?

Miscellaneous Discussion Questions

- What would you describe as your greatest strength as an executive director?
- What would you describe as your greatest weakness? How are you compensating for it?
- What skill would you most like to develop?

- Describe your present position.
- Describe your professional philosophy.
- Describe the three top-performing persons in your current organization. Why are these people productive?
- How would your co-workers describe you?
- What do you think is the most exciting thing about our position?
- What do you think is the most difficult thing about our position?
- What do you see as the hardest problem to resolve in our organization?
- What do you see as the easiest problem to resolve in our organization?
- Are there any significant reasons why you would not want to assume our executive director position?
- Are there any special circumstances that would affect your willingness to assume this position?

Briefly Summarize

Key job-related strengths of candidate, gathered from resume, interview, and supporting materials:

_____

_____

Additional information from all references:

_____

_____

Impressions from personal contact during candidate's visit(s):

_____

_____

F

PERSONAL REFERENCES

A candidate for the top staff position at a nonprofit organization should be asked for names of references. Generally, these persons should be individuals who supervised or directed the candidate in past or present employment.

No reference should be contacted without a candidate's permission. In many cases, knowledge that a candidate is looking for a new job may jeopardize his or her present position. As a general rule, references are checked after the personal interview with a candidate, if the search committee is seriously interested in the candidate.

Written and telephone responses from reference-givers each have advantages. A written reference may be better thought out and go into more detail. Telephone references can be obtained quickly and notes made of the respondents' answers. In addition, telephone interviews may provide more of a "reality check," as reference givers may be willing to provide off-the-record information. If a written reference is essential, a committee member can make telephone inquiries and ask for a written follow-up.

Whether references are written or by telephone, they should be responsive to uniform questions in specific areas. Search committees calling or writing reference sources and analyzing their responses should keep certain areas in mind. They include:

■ **The relationship of the reference source to the candidate.** Was the reference a direct supervisor? How much contact did the reference source and the candidate have? Did the reference source ever evaluate the candidate's job performance?

■ **Duties of position.** The duties of the candidate's position at the time the reference and candidate worked together should be described in operational terms. How much responsibility and authority were involved? How similar were the duties performed to those of the position to be filled?

■ **Quality of performance.** Evidence of specific accomplishments should be requested; strengths and weaknesses should be noted.

■ **Evidence of professional growth.** Do reference sources associated with the candidate's chronologically later positions note increased responsibility and authority on the part of the candidate? Are weaknesses noted by earlier reference sources still in evidence?

■ **Reasons for leaving previous position.** Were reasons for leaving positive (moved to a higher position), neutral (layoff), or negative?

Finally, if the committee wishes to discuss the reference material with the candidate, it needs to know whether the reference source will assent. References are confidential between the source and the receiver, unless the source authorizes disclosure of the information.

ABOUT THE AUTHORS

EUGENE H. FRAM is the J. Warren McClure Research Professor, College of Business, Rochester Institute of Technology. He is the author of more than 70 articles and five books about business and nonprofit issues. Dr. Fram has served as a consultant to a wide range of business organizations and as a nonprofit volunteer director, board chairman, and consultant. His previous book on nonprofit management is *Policy vs. Paper Clips: Selling the Corporate Model to Your Nonprofit Board.*

ROBERT F. PEARSE is Distinguished Lecturer in Management, College of Business, Rochester Institute of Technology. He is both a diplomate (ABPP) and a fellow (APA) in industrial/organizational psychology. Dr. Pearse specializes in leadership and organizational behavioral skill development. He designed, developed, introduced, and taught the American Management Association's *Improving Leadership Skills* course.